Reading
EXPLORER 1

Nancy Douglas

HEINLE
CENGAGE Learning™

Australia • Brazil • Japan • Korea • Mexico • Singapore • Spain • United Kingdom • United States

HEINLE
CENGAGE Learning

Reading Explorer 1
Nancy Douglas

President: Dennis Hogan
VP, National Geographic Operations: Vincent Grosso
Publisher: Andrew Robinson
Editorial Manager: Sean Bermingham
Senior Development Editor: Derek Mackrell
Editorial Assistant: Marissa Petrarca
Publisher, ELT Technology: Mac Mendelsohn
Technology Development Manager: Debie Mirtle
Technology Project Manager: Pam Prater
Asset Development Coordinator: Noah Vincelette
Director of Global Marketing: Ian Martin
Director of Content and Media Production:
Michael Burggren
Content Project Manager: Tan Jin Hock
Senior Print Buyer: Mary Beth Hennebury
Editorial Project Development (CD-ROM):
Content*Ed Publishing Solutions, LLC
National Geographic Coordinator: Leila Hishmeh
Contributing Writers: Colleen Sheils, Sue Leather
Cover/Text Designer: Page 2, LLC
Compositor: Page 2, LLC
Cover Images: (Top) Kenneth Garrett/National
Geographic Image Collection, (bottom) Sarah Leen/
National Geographic Image Collection

Credits appear on page 160, which constitutes
a continuation of the copyright page.

Acknowledgments
The Author and Publishers would like to thank the following
teaching professionals for their valuable feedback during
the development of this series.

Jamie Ahn, English Coach, Seoul; **Heidi Bundschoks**,
ITESM, Sinaloa México; **José Olavo de Amorim**, Colégio
Bandeirantes, São Paulo; **Marina Gonzalez**, Instituto
Universitario de Lenguas Modernas Pte., Buenos Aires;
Tsung-Yuan Hsiao, National Taiwan Ocean University,
Keelung; **Michael Johnson**, Muroran Institute of Technology;
Thays Ladosky, Colégio Damas, Recife; **Ahmed Mohamed
Motala**, University of Sharjah; **David Persey**, British Council,
Bangkok; **David Schneer**, ACS International, Singapore;
Atsuko Takase, Kinki University, Osaka; **Deborah E. Wilson**,
American University of Sharjah

Additional thanks to Yulia P. Boyle, Jim Burch, Michael
Colonna, and Dierdre Attardi at National Geographic
Society; and to Paul MacIntyre for his helpful comments and
suggestions.

This series is dedicated to the memory of Joe Dougherty,
who was a constant inspiration throughout its development.

For permission to use material from this text or product,
submit all requests online at **www.cengage.com/permissions**
Further permissions questions can be emailed to
permissionrequest@cengage.com

Student Book ISBN-13: 978-1-4240-2933-4
Student Book ISBN-10: 1-4240-2933-3
Student Book + Student CD-ROM ISBN-13: 978-1-4240-0637-3
Student Book + Student CD-ROM ISBN-10: 1-4240-0637-6
Student Book (US edition) ISBN-13: 978-1-4240-4362-0
Student Book (US edition) ISBN-10: 1-4240-4362-X

Heinle
20 Channel Center
Boston, Massachusetts 02210
USA

Cengage Learning is a leading provider of customized learning solutions
with office locations around the globe, including Singapore, the United
Kingdom, Australia, Mexico, Brazil, and Japan. Locate our local office at:
international.cengage.com/region

Cengage Learning products are represented in Canada by Nelson
Education, Ltd.

Visit Heinle online at **elt.heinle.com**
Visit our corporate website at **www.cengage.com**

Printed in Canada
3 4 5 6 7 – 12 11 10

☐ Contents

In **Sabinas**, **Mexico**, scientists made an amazing discovery. What did they find? **p. 86**

In May 1937 Amelia Earhart took off from **Oakland, U.S.A.**, on a round-the-world flight. What happened to her? **p. 137**

NORTH AMERICA

Movies and books have made pirates famous. But what was life like for the real pirates of the **Caribbean**? **p. 123**

Nearly 100 years ago, a lost city was found in the jungles of **Peru**. Who built the city— and why? **p. 40**

SOUTH AMERICA

Bahian samba is a dance, a rhythm, a way of life. What makes it so special? **p. 35**

New Zealand's Fiordland has been called the Eighth Wonder of the World. Why? **p. 108**

In May 2007, a very tired cyclist arrived in **Ushuaia**, **Argentina**. How far had he traveled? **p. 21**

One of the world's best-loved books comes from **Germany**. Who wrote it? **p. 89**

Smokejumpers in **Russia** have a very dangerous job. What do they do? **p. 103**

The tomb of **China**'s First Emperor has not yet been fully opened. What treasures might still be there? **p. 142**

EUROPE

ASIA

AFRICA

Gyeongju and **Kyoto** are very popular cities for tourists. Why do so many people go there? **p. 74**

In **Thailand**, you can see some elephants with very unusual skills. What can they do? **p. 15**

Dubai is one of the world's fastest-growing cities. What is the secret of its success? **p. 59**

AUSTRALIA

For nearly 4,000 years, **Giza**'s Great Pyramid was the world's tallest building. Who really built it—and why? **p. 117**

A man from **Canary Islands** is now a world-famous shoe designer. Why are his shoes so popular? **p. 65**

A radio telescope in **Australia** is listening for messages from space. Will it find life beyond earth? **p. 47**

ANTARCTICA

Explore Your World! **5**

Scope and Sequence

Unit	Theme	Lesson	Reading	Vocabulary Building	Video
1	Amazing Animals	A: Animal Intelligence B: Artistic Animals	The Incredible Dolphin Musical Elephants	Word Link: *-ance / -ence* Word Link: *-ist*	Monkey College
2	Travel and Adventure	A: Adventure Destinations B: Extreme Activities	Travel Adventure: Alaska to Argentina Extreme Destination: Vanuatu	Usage: *advice* vs. *advise* Word Partnership: *native*	Land Divers
3	Music and Festivals	A: A World of Music B: Carnival Time!	Hip-Hop Planet Brazilian Samba!	Usage: *female* vs. *woman* Word Link: *-ation / -ion*	Steel Drums
Review 1	City in the Clouds	World Heritage Spotlight: Machu Picchu, Peru		Word Link: *-tion / -sion / -ation* Word Partnership: *take*	
4	Other Worlds	A: Making Contact B: Living on the Red Planet	Life Beyond Earth? Colonies in Space	Word Partnership: *message* Word Link: *in- / im-*	The Moon
5	City Living	A: Urban Explosion B: City of the Future	City Challenges Dubai: Then and Now	Word Partnership: *traffic* Word Link: *-ful*	Living in Venice
6	Clothing and Fashion	A: From Sandal to Space Boot B: The Silk Story	More Than a Shoe? The Miracle of Silk	Word Link: *-y* Word Link: *un-*	Silk Weavers of Vietnam
Review 2	Ancient Capitals	World Heritage Spotlight: Gyeongju, Korea / Kyoto, Japan		Word Link: *in- / im- / un-* Word Partnership: *make*	

Welcome to Reading Explorer!

In this book, you'll travel the world, explore different cultures, and discover interesting topics. You'll also become a better reader!

Reading will be easier—and you'll understand more—if you ask yourself these questions:

What do I already know?
- Before you read, look at the photos, captions, and maps. Ask yourself: *What do I already know about this topic?*
- Think about the language you know—or may need to know—to understand the topic.

What do I want to learn?
- Look at the title and headings. Ask yourself: *What is this passage about? What will I learn?*
- As you read, check your predictions.

What have I learned?
- As you read, take notes. Use them to help you answer questions about the passage.
- Write down words you learn in a vocabulary notebook.

How can I learn more?
- Practice your reading skills and vocabulary in the Review Units.
- Explore the topics by watching the videos in class, or at home using the CD-ROM.

Now you're ready to explore your world!

map   headings   title   photos

caption

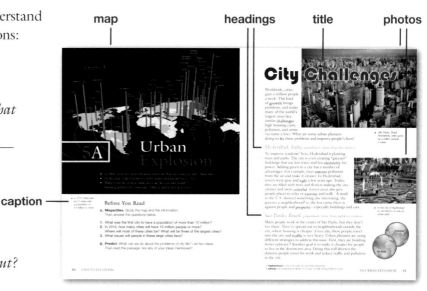

UNIT 1

Amazing Animals

Discuss these questions with a partner.

1. What can humans do that animals can't?
2. What can some animals do that humans can't?
3. What is your favorite animal? Why?

▲ A proboscis monkey and its baby jump between trees in Sabah, Malaysia.

1A

Animal Intelligence

▲ Bottlenose dolphins are social animals.

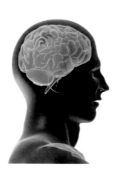

▲ A human brain

▲ A whistle

Before You Read

A. True or False. Read the sentences below, and circle **T** (True) or **F** (False). Then check your answers on page 18.

Fast Facts: The Bottlenose Dolphin

1. Dolphins are mammals (like cats, horses, and humans), not fish.   **T   F**
2. A dolphin's brain is bigger than a human's.   **T   F**
3. Dolphins communicate with each other using clicking and whistling sounds.   **T   F**
4. As adults, dolphins live by themselves.   **T   F**

B. Skim for the Main Idea. On the next page, look at the title, headings, photos, and captions. What is this reading mainly about? Circle **a**, **b**, or **c**. Then read the passage to check your answer.

   a. types of dolphins   **b.** things dolphins do   **c.** what dolphins eat

The Incredible Dolphin

1   Many people say dolphins are very **intelligent**. They seem to be able to think, understand, and learn things quickly. But are they **smart** like humans or more like cats or dogs? Dolphins use their brains differently from people. But scientists say
5   dolphin intelligence and human intelligence *are* **alike** in some ways. How?

FACT 1: Talk to Me

Like humans, every dolphin has its own "name." The name is a special whistle. Each dolphin chooses a **specific** whistle
10 for itself, usually by its first birthday. Actually, scientists think dolphins, like people, "talk" to each other about a lot of things, such as their age, their feelings, or finding food. And, like humans, dolphins use a **system** of sounds and body language to communicate. But understanding their
15 **conversations** is not easy for humans. No one "speaks dolphin" yet, but some scientists are trying to learn.

▲ Dolphins communicate using sounds and body language.

FACT 2: Let's Play

Dolphins are also social animals. They live in groups called *pods*, and they often join others from different pods to play
20 games and have fun—just like people. In fact, playing together is something only intelligent animals do.

▼ Like humans, dolphins play games together.

FACT 3: Fishermen's Helpers

Dolphins and humans are similar in another way: both make plans to get something they want. In the seas of southern
25 Brazil, for example, dolphins use an interesting **strategy** to get food. When fish are near a boat, dolphins signal[1] to the fishermen to put their nets in the water. Using this **method,** the men can catch a lot of fish. What is the **advantage** for the dolphins? Why do they **assist** the men? The dolphins get
30 to eat some of the fish.

[1] If you **signal** to someone, you make a gesture or sound to tell them something.

Reading Comprehension

A. Multiple Choice. Choose the best answer for each question.

Main Idea **1.** What is the main idea of the reading?
    a. Dolphins are very intelligent animals.
    b. There are many different types of dolphins.
    c. Some dolphins are more intelligent than humans.
    d. Dolphins are humans' favorite animals.

Detail **2.** Which sentence about dolphin language is true?
    a. A dolphin gets its name from its mother.
    b. Dolphins use language to talk about many things.
    c. Dolphins whistle, but they don't use body language.
    d. Dolphin conversation is easy to understand.

Detail **3.** Why do dolphins sometimes help fishermen?
    a. Dolphins are kind animals.
    b. So the dolphins can get food.
    c. The dolphins know the men are hungry.
    d. The fishermen ask the dolphins for help.

Reference **4.** In line 19, *others* means *other* _____.
    a. pods   b. people   c. dolphins   d. games

Vocabulary **5.** In the sentence *The dolphins get to eat some of the fish.* (line 29), what does *get to* mean?
    a. are able to   b. have to   c. should   d. want to

B. Classification. How are dolphins and humans different? How are they the same? Write the answers (a–h) in the diagram.

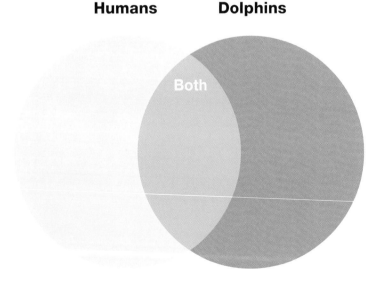

Humans   **Dolphins**

Both

a. play games in groups
b. have their own names
c. use spoken words to communicate
d. plan ways to do something
e. catch fish for food
f. communicate their feelings to each other
g. choose their own names
h. use sounds and body language to talk

Vocabulary Practice

A. Completion. Complete the information with the words from the box. One word is extra.

alike	conversation	intelligent	strategy	system

The orangutan is known for its red hair and long arms. But did you know that the orangutan is also a very **1.** _____ animal? For example, orangutans use a(n) **2.** _____ to stay dry when it rains: they take leaves from the trees and use them like an umbrella! These animals don't have a complex[1] language **3.** _____ like humans do. But today, some orangutans are learning basic sign language. Maybe, in the future, we will be able to have a simple **4.** _____ with them.

[1] complex: made up of many parts

B. Matching. Read the information below and match each word in red with a definition.

In some ways, animal and human intelligence are alike. But just how smart are some animals? Scientists in Japan wanted to study memory in humans and chimps. They used this method: they showed a group of college students and five-year-old chimps the numbers 1 to 9 in different places on a computer screen, but only for a short while. The test was to remember the specific position of the numbers in the correct order. Every time, the chimps were faster than the students. Why? Did someone assist the chimps? No, but the animals probably had an important advantage: they're young. As both humans and animals get older, memory gets worse. The chimps also had another advantage: humans seem to use more of their brain for language and less for memory.

1. a way of doing something: _____
2. help: _____
3. similar: _____
4. something that helps you succeed: _____
5. exact: _____
6. intelligent: _____

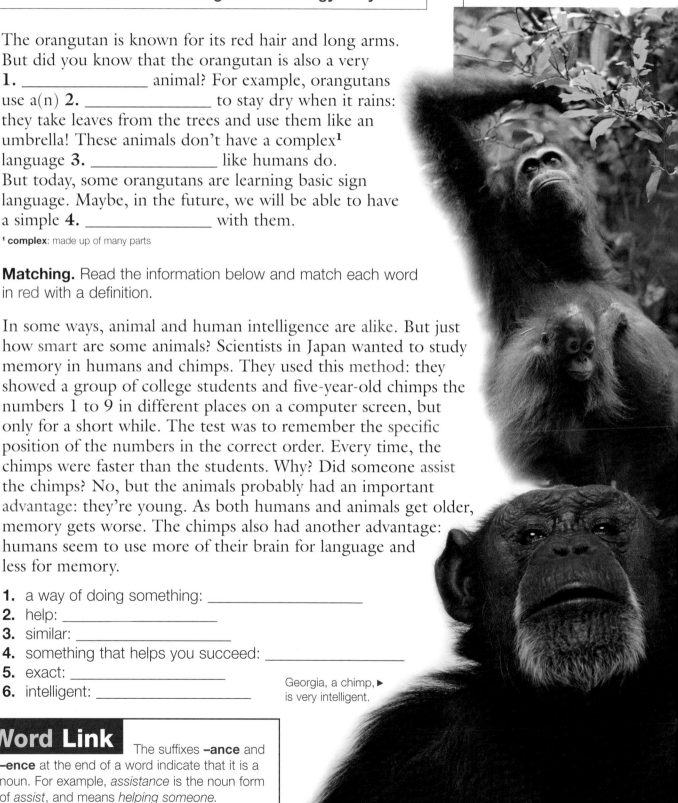

Georgia, a chimp, ▶ is very intelligent.

> **Word Link** The suffixes **–ance** and **–ence** at the end of a word indicate that it is a noun. For example, *assistance* is the noun form of *assist*, and means *helping someone*.

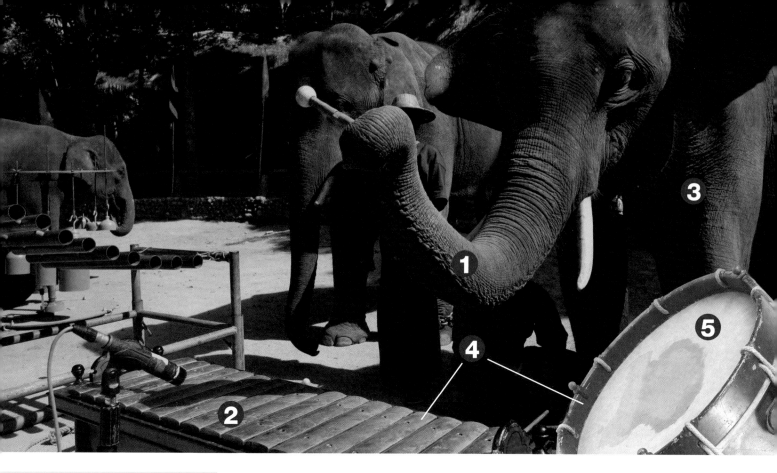

1B Artistic Animals

Before You Read

A. Labeling. Read the information below. Then label the numbered items in the picture with the words in blue.

Can an elephant make music? Some people might say "no," but the animals in the photo are musicians. Each elephant uses its trunk to play different instruments, like the **drum** or the **xylophone**.

① _____   **④** _____

② _____   **⑤** _____

③ _____

B. Predict. Which of these do you think elephants can do? Check (✔) your answer(s). Then read the information on the next page to check your idea(s).

☐ paint   ☐ play music   ☐ cook food   ☐ play soccer

Musical Elephants

1   In the town of Lampang in northern Thailand, there is an unusual[1] group of musicians. They play many different kinds of
5   music—everything from traditional Thai songs to music by Beethoven. Both children and adults love this group. What makes them so **popular**? Is it their music? Their
10 looks?[2] Yes, it's both of these things, but it's also something else: they're elephants.

These musical elephants started at the Thai Elephant Conservation Center (TECC) in Lampang.
15 The TECC protects elephants. It teaches people to understand and care for these **huge**, but **gentle**, animals. And, like many zoos around the world, the TECC **encourages** elephants to paint.

▲ Sangduen Chailert helps elephants at a nature park near Chiang Mai, Thailand.

Richard Lair works with the TECC. He knows a lot about
20 elephants. He says some of the animals' paintings are very good. But, in fact, elephants hear better than they see. And so he had an idea: if elephants are intelligent and they have good hearing, maybe they can play music. To test his idea, Lair and a friend started the Thai Elephant Orchestra.[3] During a
25 **performance**, the elephants play a variety of instruments, including the drums and the xylophone. The animals also use their voices and trunks to make sounds.

But can elephants really make music **properly**? Yes, says Lair. They're very **creative**. Humans encourage the animals to
30 play, but the elephants make their own songs; they don't just copy their **trainers** or other people. There are now CDs of the group's music, which **earn** money for the TECC. And the music these **artists** create is pretty amazing.

---

[1] If something is **unusual**, it does not happen very often or you do not see it or hear it very often.
[2] When you refer to someone's **looks**, you are referring to how beautiful or ugly they are.
[3] An **orchestra** is a large group of musicians who play a variety of instruments together.

Reading Comprehension

A. Multiple Choice. Choose the best answer for each question.

Gist **1.** Another title for this reading could be _____.
a. Teaching Elephants to Paint
b. Elephants in Danger
c. TECC Trainers
d. An Unusual Orchestra

Detail **2.** The elephants at the TECC _____.
a. see better than they hear
b. are able to paint
c. copy humans to play music
d. make their own instuments

Detail **3.** Why did Richard Lair start the Thai Elephant Orchestra?
a. He had heard the elephants playing music.
b. He needed to make money for the TECC.
c. He believed elephants could play music.
d. He wanted to be on TV in Thailand.

Vocabulary **4.** In line 25, what does *a variety of* mean?
a. the same kind of   b. many different   c. two types of   d. too many

Paraphrase **5.** Read the last sentence in the passage again. What does it mean?
a. The elephants play great music.
b. Human artists now play with the elephants.
c. The elephants are very beautiful.
d. Human musicians want to copy the elephants' songs.

B. Matching. What is the main idea of each paragraph in the reading?
Match a heading (a–e) with the correct paragraph (1–4). One heading is extra.

Paragraph	Heading
1. _____	**a.** One man's idea: The Elephant Orchestra
2. _____	**b.** An unusual group of musicians
3. _____	**c.** Why do animals like music?
4. _____	**d.** The elephants really can play music!
	e. The work of the TECC

Phong, an elephant at the TECC, can play the xylophone with his trunk. ▼

Vocabulary Practice

A. Completion. Complete the information with words from the box. One word is extra.

artists	popular
earn	trainers
encourage	creative

Many elephants can paint. In fact, elephants in zoos sometimes draw on the ground with a stick. Seeing this, some elephant **1.** _____ show elephants how to hold a paintbrush, and **2.** _____ the elephants to choose colors and paint. Of course, not every painting is good. Just like humans, only some elephants are very **3.** _____. Now, an online gallery sells paintings by these elephant **4.** _____. By doing this, the gallery hopes to **5.** _____ money to protect elephants.

▲ This painting, called "Green Symphony," was painted by Phong, an elephant at the Royal Thai Conservation Center.
Courtesy of NOVICA.COM

B. Words in Context. Complete each sentence with the best answer.

1. A gentle person _____ hurt an animal.
   a. wouldn't   b. would

2. A huge animal is very _____.
   a. large   b. small

3. If something is popular, _____ people like it.
   a. a lot of   b. very few

4. If you do something properly, you do it _____.
   a. poorly   b. correctly

5. An example of a musical performance is _____.
   a. an orchestra playing music by Mozart
   b. a teacher explaining how to read music

Word Link We can add **–ist** to words to form nouns. These nouns often describe jobs, for example, *artist* and *scientist*.

Monkey College

LAOS

MYANMAR
(BURMA)

THAILAND

★Bangkok   CAMBODIA

Gulf
of
Thailand

Surat Thani

ASIA

THAILAND

INDIAN
OCEAN

MALAYSIA

A. Preview. Match each word in the box with an item in the picture.

coconut	monkey	rope	trainer

1._____

2._____

3._____

4._____

 B. Summarize. Watch the video, *Monkey College*.
Then complete the summary below using the correct form
of words from the box. Two words are extra.

advantage	encourage	intelligent	popular
assistance	gentle	method	trainer
earn	huge	perform	

Some monkeys are so **1.** _____ they get to go to
school! Somporn Saewkwo is a(n) **2.** _____ at
Thailand's Monkey Training College in Surat Thani. He uses a
creative way to teach monkeys a very important job—how to pick
coconuts from tall trees. First, he holds the monkey's hands. He
shows the animal how to spin (turn) a coconut to take it from a tree.
Later, Saewkwo takes the monkey to a high tree and he
3. _____ the animal to climb up and pick the fruit.
The monkey wears a rope. Using this, Saewkwo can direct the
animal from the ground. The **4.** _____ of using this
5. _____ is that the trainer doesn't have to climb a tree.

Coconuts are very **6.** _____ in Thailand: they are
used in many foods. A(n) **7.** _____ number of
coconuts are picked each month (almost two million!). Farmers can
8. _____ a lot of money from this fruit. But they
probably couldn't do this without **9.** _____ from
their helpers—the monkeys. Because these animals are so
important, most are treated well by farmers.

C. Think About It.

1. How does Somporn
Saewkwo teach
the monkeys?
2. Do you think
monkeys are
more or less
intelligent than other
animals you read
about in this unit?
Why?

 To learn more about
amazing animals, visit
elt.heinle.com/explorer

18 Unit 1 Amazing Animals

Answers to Before You Read quiz on page 10:
1. T; 2. T; 3. T; 4. F. Most bottlenose dolphins live in groups, called *pods*.

UNIT 2

Travel and Adventure

Discuss these questions with a partner.

1. When you travel, what kinds of activities do you like to do?
2. What places in the world would you most like to visit? Why?
3. What is the most adventurous thing that you've ever done?

▲ A scientist lowers himself into one of the world's
largest caves, Majlis al Jinn, in Oman.

19

2A Adventure Destinations

Before You Read

A. Completion. Look at the photos and read about each place. Then complete each description with a word from the box.

Top Adventure Travel Destinations

camp	cruise	hike	swim

MOUNTAIN Colombia

Travel along Colombia's "coffee highway" and _____ through beautiful mountain villages in the Andes.

DESERT Mongolia

Travel through its wide-open desert. Bring a tent and _____ outdoors under the sky at night. It's an amazing experience!

FOREST Senegal

Take a riverboat _____ and see this country's natural wonders, like mangrove forests full of animal life.

BEACH Albania

Visit the country's beautiful coastal towns, walk along white-sand beaches, and _____ in the blue waters of the Ionian Sea.

B. Scan. You are going to read about two friends' travel adventure. Quickly scan the reading to answer the questions below. Then read again to check your answers.

1. Where did they start and end their trip? How did they travel?
2. How many kilometers (or miles) did they travel?

Travel Adventure:
Alaska to Argentina

Prudhoe Bay, AL

San Francisco, CA

Mexico City, Mexico

Panama City, Panama

La Paz, Bolivia

Ushuaia, Argentina

1 **Many people dream of going on a great travel adventure. Most of us keep dreaming; others make it happen . . .**

Gregg Bleakney's dream was to travel the Americas from top to bottom. He got the idea after he finished a 1,600 kilometer
5 (1,000 mile) bike ride. Gregg's friend, Brooks Allen, was also a cyclist.[1] The two friends talked and slowly **formed** a plan: they would travel from Alaska to Argentina—by bike.

To pay for the **trip**, Gregg and Brooks worked and saved their money for years. Once they were on the road, they
10 often camped outdoors or stayed in hostels.[2] In many places, local people opened their homes to the two friends and gave them food.

During their trip, Gregg and Brooks cycled through deserts, rainforests, and mountains. They visited modern cities and
15 **ancient** ruins[3] such as Machu Picchu in Peru. And everywhere they went, they met other cyclists from all over the world.

In May 2007—two years, twelve countries, and over 30,500 km (19,000 miles) later—Gregg **eventually** reached Ushuaia, Argentina, the southernmost city in the world. (Near
20 Guatemala, Brooks had to return to the U.S., and Gregg continued without him.)

The trip taught both men a lot about traveling, **especially** if you travel **abroad**. What did they learn? Here is some of Gregg's **advice**:

25 **Travel light.** The less **baggage** you have, the less you'll worry about.

Be flexible. Don't plan everything. Then you'll be more **relaxed** and happy, especially if there are problems.

30 **Be polite.** As one traveller told Gregg, "Always remember that nobody wants to fight, cheat, or rob[4] a nice guy."

▲ Gregg and Brooks (right) cycle past ruins in Tikal National Park, Guatemala.

[1] A **cyclist** is someone who rides a bicycle.
[2] A **hostel** is a cheap place to stay and sleep when traveling.
[3] The **ruins** of something are the parts of it that remain after it has been broken.
[4] If someone is **robbed**, they have money or property stolen from them.

Reading Comprehension

A. Multiple Choice. Choose the best answer for each question.

Gist **1.** Another title for this reading could be _____.
   a. Cycling the Americas from Top to Bottom
   b. The Southernmost City in the World
   c. Things to See and Do in Alaska and Argentina
   d. Argentina: The Land of Adventure

Detail **2.** Which sentence about Gregg and Brooks' trip is NOT true?
   a. To pay for the trip, they saved their money and traveled cheaply on the road.
   b. Only Gregg made the complete trip from Alaska to Argentina.
   c. During their trip, they met people from all over the world.
   d. In Guatemala, Gregg got sick and went back to the U.S.A.

Reference **3.** In line 12, *them* means _____.
   a. the local people   c. other cyclists
   b. Gregg and Brooks   d. their friends

Vocabulary **4.** Which of these words or phrases is most similar in meaning to *flexible* in line 27?
   a. able to change easily   c. well-planned
   b. careful   d. difficult

Inference **5.** Which statement would Gregg most likely agree with?
   a. In other countries, only stay in hotels or with people you know.
   b. Plan every part of your trip so you can relax.
   c. When abroad, learn how to say "thank you" in the local language.
   d. Bring a lot with you on your trip so you don't have to buy anything.

B. Sequencing. Put the events below in order from 1–6. Then retell this story to a partner.

_____ Gregg and Brooks start their trip in Prudhoe Bay, Alaska.
_____ Gregg reaches Ushuaia, Argentina.
_____ Gregg goes on a 1,000-mile bike ride.
_____ Gregg and his friend Brooks talk about biking from Alaska to Argentina.
_____ Brooks returns to the U.S.A. Gregg continues without him.
_____ Gregg and Brooks work to save money.

Vocabulary Practice

A. Definitions. Read the information below. Then match each word in red with its definition.

Are you planning to travel **abroad?** If you're looking for both beauty and adventure, think about visiting Patagonia. It is an area that is shared by both Chile and Argentina. Here are two places you shouldn't miss:

- Cave of the Hands: These **ancient** cave paintings were done 9,500–13,000 years ago by some of Patagonia's earliest people.

- Glaciers National Park is a great place for hiking and mountain climbing. See blue lakes and white glaciers— huge rivers of ice—that were **formed** millions of years ago.

1. very old _____
2. made, created _____
3. overseas, in another country _____

B. Completion. Complete the information with words from the box. One word is extra.

advice	especially	polite	trip
baggage	eventually	relax	

A lot of smart people make mistakes when they go hiking. Here's some **1.** _____ that can help you stay safe:

Before you start, tell someone where you are going and for how long, **2.** _____ if you are going alone.

No one likes to carry a lot of **3.** _____.
But it's important to take certain things on your
4. _____: water, extra clothing, and a cell phone.

If you get lost or hurt, you should "S.T.O.P." This means:
  Stop: try to **5.** _____ and stay calm.
  Think about your situation.
  Observe: look around and notice where you are.
  Plan what to do next.
Also, it's important to stay in one place. Someone will
6. _____ look for you.

Usage

Advice is a noun, and the *c* is pronounced like the *ss* in *less*; **advise** is a verb, and the *s* is pronounced like the *z* in *size*: *Jenny advised Alan not to give people advice!*

2B Extreme Activities

Before You Read

The South Pacific

Home to some of the best water and adventure sports in the world

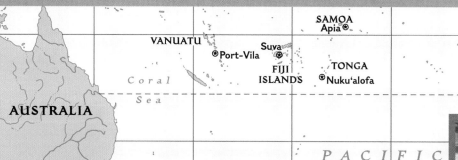

- Tonga has great waves, and (a) **surfing** is popular here.
- Vanuatu has some of the best sea (b) **kayaking** in the world.
- In New Zealand—"The Adventure Capital of the World"— you can do everything from (c) **bungee jumping** to (d) **snorkeling** with the fish.

A. Matching. Look at the map and read the information.

1. Which countries are described? Find and circle them on the map.

2. Match the words in blue (a–d) with the sport pictured.

B. Skim for the Main Idea. On the next page, look quickly at the title, headings, photos, and captions. Which word best describes the activites on Vanuatu? Circle **a**, **b**, or **c**. Then read the passage to check your answer.

    a. expensive   **b.** dangerous   **c.** relaxing

Extreme Destination:
VANUATU

▲ Yasur Volcano,
Tanna Island,
Vanuatu

1 Vanuatu is an island nation in the South Pacific. It is also one of the smallest countries in the world. But for those interested in adventure and sport, there is a lot to do. Some of the best snorkeling and sea kayaking can be found here. Vanuatu's islands also offer visitors
5 two of the most exciting—and dangerous—activities in the world: volcano surfing and land diving.

Volcano Surfing

On Tanna Island, Mount Yasur rises 300 meters (1,000 feet) into the sky. Yasur is an active volcano, and it erupts[1] almost every day,
10 sometimes several times a day. For **centuries**, both island locals and visitors have climbed this mountain to visit the top. Recently, people have also started climbing Yasur to surf the volcano.
In some ways, volcano surfing is like surfing in the sea, but in other ways it's very different. A volcano surfer's **goal** is to **escape** the
15 erupting volcano—without getting **hit** by flying rocks! It's fast, fun, and dangerous—the perfect **extreme** sport.

Land Diving

Most people are **familiar** with bungee jumping, but did you know bungee jumping started on Pentecost Island in Vanuatu and is
20 almost fifteen centuries old? The original activity, called land diving, is part of a **religious** ceremony.[2] A man **ties** tree vines[3] to his legs. He then jumps head-first from a high tower. The goal: to touch the earth with the top of his head—without breaking the vine and hitting the ground hard. Every spring, island **natives** (men only)
25 still perform this amazing test of **strength**.

▲ A man jumps
from a tower on
Pentecost Island.

[1] When a volcano **erupts,** it throws out hot rock called *lava*.
[2] A **ceremony** is a formal event such as a wedding.
[3] A **vine** is a plant that grows up or over things.

Tanna women paint ▲
their faces and dress
in special clothes for
a ceremony.

Reading Comprehension

A. Multiple Choice. Choose the best answer for each question.

Purpose **1.** What is the purpose of this reading?
   a. to encourage people not to do dangerous sports
   b. to explain what volcano surfing and land diving are
   c. to talk about the world's best volcano surfer and land diver
   d. to compare activities in Vanuatu with sports in New Zealand

Detail **2.** Which sentence about Mount Yasur is true?
   a. It is no longer active.   c. People have been climbing it for a long time.
   b. It gets a lot of snow.   d. It's on Pentecost Island.

Detail **3.** Land diving _____.
   a. was first called "bungee jumping"
   b. came to Vanuatu from another country
   c. is less popular today than in the past
   d. is a traditional activity in Vanuatu

Reference **4.** In line 2, what does *those* refer to?
   a. people   b. countries   c. activities   d. islands

Vocabulary **5.** In line 23, what does *the earth* mean?
   a. the people   b. the ground   c. the tower   d. the world

B. Classification. Match each answer (a–g) with the activity it describes.

Volcano surfing   **Land diving**

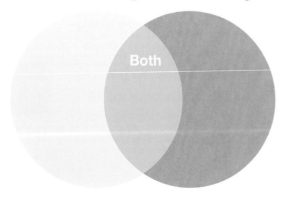

Both

a. is only done by men
b. is a new sport
c. is dangerous because of flying rocks
d. is a very old activity
e. was first done on Pentecost Island
f. is similar to a popular water sport
g. is a very fast activity

Vocabulary Practice

A. Completion. Complete the information with the correct form of words from the box. One word is extra.

century	extreme	goal	native	strength
escape	familiar	hit	religious	tie

The Festival of San Fermín
Where: the city of Pamplona in northern Spain
When: early July, for nine days
What happens: Every day, there are special events: music, dances, and **1.** _____ ceremonies. But the part of the festival that most people are **2.** _____ with is "the running of the bulls." Every morning, a group of bulls runs down a city street. Hundreds of people run in front of the animals. Runners wear white; they also **3.** _____ a red scarf around their bodies. The run lasts three minutes. A runner's **4.** _____ is to **5.** _____ from the bulls without falling or getting **6.** _____ by them. Running with the bulls started in Spain in the 13th **7.** _____, and is still very popular today. Pamplona **8.** _____ and visitors from all over the world join in. The run is very dangerous. So why do people do it? For some runners, it is a test of **9.** _____. For others, the run makes them feel alive.

▲ People wearing red and white run from the bulls in Pamplona, Spain.

B. Definitions. Use the words in the box in **A** to complete the definitions.

1. A(n) _____ is 100 years.
2. If you _____ from something, you run away from it.
3. A(n) _____ is an aim or something you are trying to do.
4. A(n) _____ of somewhere is from that place.
5. If you touch someone or something very hard, you _____ them.
6. If you are _____ with something, you know or understand it well.
7. If you _____ two things together, you bring them together with a knot.

Word Partnership Use *native* with: native **country**, native **land**, native **language**, native **tongue**.

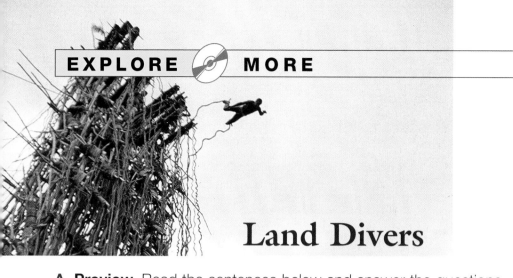

Land Divers

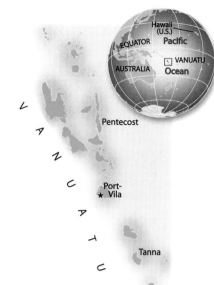

A. Preview. Read the sentences below and answer the questions.

The natives of Vanuatu are led by a **chief.**
Land diving is very dangerous, so you need to be very **brave** to do it.

1. A *chief* is _____.
   a. an important person   b. an important place

2. Someone who is *brave* is _____ to do dangerous things.
   a. afraid   b. not afraid

B. Summarize. Watch the video, *Land Divers*. Then complete the summary below with the correct form of words from the box. Two words are extra.

advice	eventually	goal	relax
century	extreme	hit	religious
especially	form	native	tie

Modern bungee jumping started in New Zealand. But this
1. _____ sport actually started about a(n)
2. _____ ago as a(n) **3.** _____
ceremony on Pentecost Island. In the local language, it is called
Nagol. This means "land diving." One islander has some
4. _____ for divers: It's important to
5. _____ when you are on the tower. Land
diving can be very dangerous, **6.** _____ if you are
nervous. The last time a diver died was in 1974. But every year,
people **7.** _____ the ground hard and they get
hurt. People from other countries can watch, but only Vanuatu
8. _____ can join in Nagol. For a National
Geographic video, the chief allowed one brave diver to
9. _____ a camera to his leg. His
10. _____ was to use the camera to film his jump.
On his second jump the diver's vine broke, but he was not hurt.
"I'm a lucky man!" he later said.

C. Think About It.

1. Why do you think the native people of Pentecost Island do land diving?

2. In your opinion, which activity in this unit is the most dangerous? Which would you like to try?

To learn more about travel and adventure, visit elt.heinle.com/explorer

UNIT 3

Music and Festivals

Discuss these questions with a partner.

1. What is your favorite kind of music? Who is your favorite artist or group?
2. Have you ever been to a concert or music festival? Who did you see?
3. Is your country famous for any music or festivals?

▲ Painted dancers enjoy the rhythms of a street festival in Bahia, Brazil.

1600
1700
1800
1900
1910
1920
1930
1940
1950
1960
1970
1980
1990
2000

From Africa to the World

3A A World of Music

1600 West African storytellers, called *griots*, use spoken words and music to tell stories. Africans brought to the Americas as **slaves** continue this tradition.

1800 Blues: By the mid 1860s, blacks are no longer slaves in the U.S.A., but many still have difficult lives. People sing blues songs about life's **hardships** to a slow, musical **rhythm**.

1920 Jazz; Samba (Brazil)

1940 Rhythm and Blues (R&B)

◄ Keb Mo', a popular blues musician, performs at the New Orleans Jazz and Heritage Festival.

▲ A modern-day griot performs with another musician on a beach in Senegal.

1950 By the early 1950s, a new type of R&B becomes popular in the U.S. White **teenagers** call this music "rock and roll."

1970 Reggae (Jamaica). Hip-hop starts in New York City.

Mid 1970s A DJ uses turntables as musical instruments while a singer "raps" with the music.

Today International hip-hop

Before You Read

A. Matching. Read the information above and match each word in **blue** with its definition.

1. _____ a regular series of sounds or movements
2. _____ people from 13 to 19 years old
3. _____ things that are difficult in life
4. _____ people who are owned by other people

B. Skim for the Main Idea. On the next page, look at the title, headings, and first paragraph. What is the passage mainly about? Circle **a, b,** or **c.** Then read the passage to check your answer.

a. Famous hip-hop artists   **c.** Hip-hop in two countries
b. The history of hip-hop

Hip-Hop Planet

1   Hip-hop started in New York City in the 1970s. Today, many countries have their own local hip-hop scenes.[1] Artists from different **backgrounds** rap about everything from cars and designer clothes to social **issues**. Here are two examples.

Dakar, Senegal

5   Assane N'Diaye, 19, loves hip-hop music. He grew up in a small fishing village in Senegal. For a time, he was popular as a DJ in **clubs** in Dakar, the capital city of Senegal.

    Today, Assane lives in his village again. He has formed a
10 rap group with other family members. They rap about their lives as village fishermen, and about working long, hard days and earning almost no money. Many people in their **audience** can understand these things. "Rap," Assane says, "doesn't **belong** to American culture. It belongs here. It has
15 always existed here, because of our pain and our hardships ..."

    Assane dreams of making a CD and having a better life. **Despite** his hardships, the music gives Assane hope.

The Czech Republic

    Europe is home to 8–12 million Roma—a group of people
20 often called "gypsies." Many Roma are poor. In some places, they also **face** discrimination.[2]

    Now some Roma teenagers are using hip-hop to teach tolerance.[3] In the Czech Republic, Roma teens meet for a hip-hop class called "Rap for **Peace** Hip-Hop." Their instructor
25 is Shameema Williams. She is a member of the all-**female** rap group Godessa, from South Africa.

    In the lessons, the teens learn to write rap music and use it to teach others about Roma culture. These teens, Shameema believes, can use the music to change their lives and other
30 people's **attitudes**. "Use your creative energy and see what the possibilities[4] are," she says.

[1] You can refer to an area of activity as a **scene**, for example, an art or music scene.
[2] **Discrimination** means treating a person or group of people less fairly or less well than others.
[3] **Tolerance** means accepting different people, religions, beliefs, etc.
[4] **Possibilities** are choices, things you can do.

Reading Comprehension

A. Multiple Choice. Choose the best answer for each question.

Purpose **1.** What is the purpose of this reading?
    a. to compare American and African rap music
    b. to say why some people do not like rap music
    c. to describe different hip-hop scenes
    d. to explain how hip-hop started

Detail **2.** Assane N'Diaye _____.
    a. only likes American rap music
    b. is going to move to the U.S.A.
    c. has already made several CDs
    d. lives in a small village

Inference **3.** Which statement would Assane N'Diaye most likely agree with?
    a. The best rappers are from the U.S.A.
    b. Rap music is a part of Senegal.
    c. Rap music came to Africa recently.
    d. Many Africans don't understand rap music.

Detail **4.** Which sentence about the Roma teenagers is NOT true?
    a. They are using music to teach people about their culture.
    b. In some places, they are disliked because they are Roma.
    c. They are taking a hip-hop class.
    d. Most of them are from South Africa.

Vocabulary **5.** In line 24, what does the word *instructor* mean?
    a. DJ   b. classmate   c. member   d. teacher

B. Classification. Match each answer (a–e) with the person it describes.

Assane N'Diaye   **Shameema Williams**

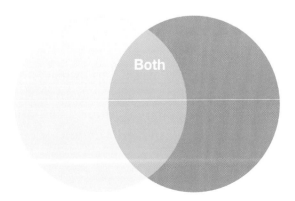

a. helps students write rap music
b. raps about life in a small village
c. was a DJ
d. is a member of a South African rap group
e. believes rap music can make life better

Vocabulary Practice

A. Completion. Complete the information below using the correct forms of the words in red.

Hip-hop started on the streets and in the **clubs** of New York City. **Despite** this, hip-hop's look and sound don't **belong** to the United States only. The music changes everywhere you go. A person from one **background**—for example, a Moroccan man living in Paris—might rap about one thing. But another person (for example, a **female** musician from Los Angeles) will rap about something different.

1. Shameema Williams is a(n) _____ rap artist.

2. If something _____ to you, you own it.

3. A _____ is a place where you can listen to music and dance.

4. Your _____ is information about you: where you come from, etc.

5. _____ being a quite new form of music, hip hop is very popular worldwide.

B. Completion. Complete the information using the correct forms of words from the box.

attitude	audience	background	face	issue	peace

The Palestinian group DAM raps in several languages, including English and Arabic. The group's music focuses on different social **1.** _____. For example, they sing about the problems that women and young people **2.** _____. They also talk about the need for **3.** _____ and tolerance. The members of DAM want to change people's **4.** _____—to help people think differently about certain things. Today, the group performs for **5.** _____ in many countries.

Usage *Female* is commonly used as an adjective, but can also be a noun; in everyday conversation, *women* usually is more polite than *females*.

▲ Members of the rap group DAM

3B Carnival Time!

Before You Read

A. Discussion. Read the information below. How are the four festivals similar? How are they different?

Every year in February or March, people in many countries celebrate Carnival. This festival can last for several days. Here are four of the biggest Carnival festivals.

New Orleans
Carnival here is called *Mardi Gras* (French for "Fat Tuesday"). There are large parades with people in costumes, and the sound of jazz music fills the streets.

Venice
"Carnevale" probably started here in the 12th century. Today, people wearing costumes parade through the streets and travel by gondola (a type of boat) around the city.

Rio de Janeiro
Rio's "Carnaval" is one of the largest festivals in the world. The energetic beat of samba—the music of Brazil—is everywhere.

Port-of-Spain
During Carnival season, people dance to the rhythm of Trinidad's native music, *soca*. The festival ends with two days of colorful parades.

B. Skim for the Main Idea. Quickly skim the passage on the next page. What is the passage mainly about? Circle **a, b,** or **c.** Then read the passage to check your answer.

a. a musical instrument   **b.** a type of music   **c.** a reggae artist

Brazilian Samba!

Salvador (Bahia), Brazil

1　Samba is one of Brazil's most popular music and dance styles. In many ways, it is a symbol[1] of the country itself. In the words of one of modern samba's main artists, Seu Jorge, "Samba is our truth, our peculiarity[2] . . . and our flag." When

5　people today hear the word *samba*, they often think of the festival of Carnaval and the city of Rio de Janeiro. But there are many different types of samba, and these styles **differ** throughout Brazil.

"Samba is our truth, . . . our flag."
Seu Jorge

Samba Reggae

10　Today, one of the most popular types of samba comes from Bahia, a state in the eastern part of the country. It's called *samba reggae*. From the 16th to 18th centuries, over three million Africans were brought to Brazil to work as slaves. Today in Bahia, 80 percent of the **population** is black.

15　Samba from this **region** of Brazil is **heavily influenced** by African rhythms. Modern samba reggae is a **mix** of Rio samba, African drumbeats, and Jamaican reggae. It's a bit slower than Rio samba, and is usually performed in large groups—sometimes with over 200 drums playing at one time!

20　Bahia's most famous drumming group is Olodum. Many say the group **invented** the samba reggae sound. But Olodum is not only a musical group. Its members have also created local **organizations** to help

25　young people and the poor. Every year in the city of Salvador in Bahia, the **lively** sounds of samba reggae **fill** the streets during Carnaval—one of the world's greatest parties.

▼ A group of Bahian musicians performs in Salvador, Brazil.

[1] A **symbol** is a thing that represents something else. For example, a flag is a symbol of a country.

[2] A **peculiarity** is something that belongs to or relates to only one person or thing.

Reading Comprehension

A. Multiple Choice. Choose the best answer for each question.

Main Idea **1.** What is the main idea of this reading?
   a. The Rio Carnaval is the most important festival in Brazil.
   b. Samba reggae is an important type of music in Brazil.
   c. Rio samba is very popular all over the world.
   d. Samba is a type of African music.

Detail **2.** Samba reggae _____.
   a. is most popular in Rio de Janeiro
   b. is faster and more energetic than Rio samba
   c. is a mix of different kinds of music
   d. started in Jamaica

Detail **3.** Olodum is _____.
   a. a samba reggae group   c. a well-known samba dancer
   b. a musical instrument   d. a town in Bahia

Paraphrase **4.** What does *Samba from this region of Brazil is heavily influenced by African rhythms.* (line 15) mean?
   a. Samba is usually played by African musicians.
   b. African music was important in creating Bahian samba.
   c. Brazilian samba is very different from African music.
   d. African music is increasingly popular in Bahia.

Reference **5.** We can change the word *It* in line 17 to _____.
   a. Samba reggae   b. Rio samba   c. Jamaican reggae   d. African music

B. Summary. Complete the diagram below with words from the reading.

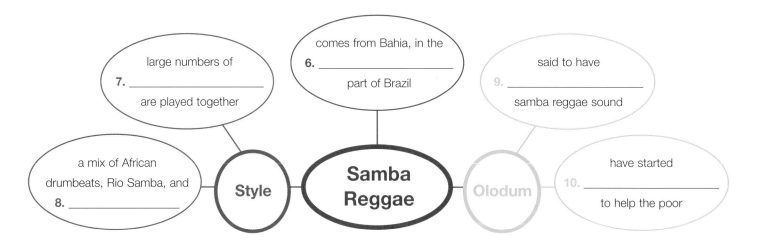

Vocabulary Practice

▲ Carlinhos Brown is one of Brazil's most popular musicians.

A. Completion. Complete the information with the correct form of words from the box. One word is extra.

organization	lively
differ	influence
mix	region

A native of Salvador, Bahia, Carlinhos Brown is one of Brazil's best-known musicians. His music is a
1. _____ of samba reggae and pop music, and is very 2. _____ and fun. And like other artists
from the Bahia 3. _____, many of Brown's songs have been 4. _____ by African drumming rhythms.

For more than 20 years, Brown has been a songwriter, musician, and singer. In the 1990s, he also started a non-profit[1] 5. _____, the Pracatum Music School. The school provides free education for poor children in Salvador, Bahia.

[1] **Non-profit** means not for making money.

B. Words in Context. Complete each sentence with the best answer.

1. If two things differ, they _____ alike.
   a. are   b. are not

2. The population of Bahia is about _____.
   a. 14 million people   b. 565,000 square kilometers
                              (218,000 square miles)

3. If a room is filled with people, the room has _____ people in it.
   a. a lot of   b. very few

4. If a person invents something, he or she _____ it.
   a. copies   b. creates

5. If it rains heavily during May and June, it rains _____.
   a. a lot   b. very slowly

Word Link   We can add **–ation** or **–ion** to verbs to form nouns (for example, *organize + ation = organization; populate + ion = population*). These nouns describe an action or a state of being.

Steel Drums

A. Preview. Look at the photos and read the captions. How do you think steel drums are made?

Oil drum: ▸
An oil drum is a large container that holds oil.

Trinidad and Tobago

 B. Summarize. Watch the video, *Steel Drums*. Then complete the summary below using the correct form of words from the box. Two words are extra.

background	face	invent	region
belong to	fill	lively	
despite	influence	organization	

▲ **Steel drum:**
A steel drum is a musical instrument.

Trinidad and Tobago is home to a(n) **1.** _____ kind of music. The sound of the steelband drum (called *pan* by the locals) **2.** _____ the air of this island nation and brings people of different **3.** _____ together. The steelband sound comes from Trinidad and Tobago and was **4.** _____ in the 20th century. How was it created? Trinidad produces oil. During the 1940s, people began using old oil drums as musical instruments. The steelband sound has **5.** _____ all kinds of music in Trinidad and throughout the Caribbean **6.** _____. Most steelband players do not read music. **7.** _____ this, they still produce amazing sounds. They play music by ear until they get a song right. For the people of Trinidad, the steelband is more than an instrument. It is part of their culture. Steelband music **8.** _____ the people of Trinidad and Tobago, but they want to share it with the world!

C. Think About It.

1. Most steelband drummers "play music by ear." What does this mean?

2. How is steelband music similar to or different from other music discussed in this unit?

 To learn more about music and festivals, visit elt.heinle.com/explorer

A. Crossword. Use the definitions below to complete the missing words.

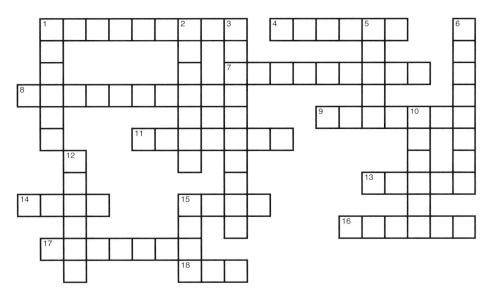

Across
1. something that helps you succeed
4. to help
7. to give hope or support to someone
8. the number of people who live in a place
9. very much; furthest
11. a period of 100 years
13. a state of calm
14. very large
15. to make something full
16. to create something for the first time
17. well liked by people
18. to bring two or more things together into one

Down
1. in a foreign country
2. very old
3. finally
5. intelligent
6. the people who watch or listen to a movie, play, or concert
10. to run away from someone or something
12. an area in a country or part of the world
15. to begin to exist; to create

B. Notes Completion. Scan the information on pages 40–41 to complete the notes.

Field Notes

Site: Machu Picchu

Location: high in the _____ mountains, Peru

Information:
- built in year _____ by _____ people
- population ranged from _____ to more than _____
- used mainly as a _____ center; only entrance was by the _____
- water brought by system of _____ and _____
- 1911: found by an explorer named _____
- now _____ tourists can visit each day
- became World Heritage Site in _____

City in the Clouds

Site: **Machu Picchu**

Location: **Peru**

Category: **Cultural**

Status: **World Heritage Site since 1983**

3

2

1

This artist's view shows Machu Picchu 500 years ago, during a festival for the sun god.

❶ **South Gate** This narrow entrance was the only way into Machu Picchu.

❷ **Warehouse** This huge building was filled with potatoes, corn, and other food, brought in by llamas.

❸ **Intiwatana** This building—made from a large rock—was formed to look like a nearby mountain. An audience at the top of the stairs is praying to the sun god in a ceremony known as *Intiraymi*.

❹ **Royal Residence** Inca people belonging to royal families probably lived in this house, where they enjoyed the advantage of having their own garden and bathroom.

❺ **Temple of the Sun** This circular temple has a window especially for the sun to shine through during the mid-winter festival.

❻ **Canal and Fountains** The Inca people invented a water system using canals and fountains, which provided drinking water for the whole population.

4

5

6

Glossary

canal: a long, narrow, man-made stretch of water

fountain: a jet of water forced into the air by a pump

temple: a building where people pray to or worship a god or gods

The Lost City

The Inca people built **Machu Picchu** in about 1450, at a place high in the Andes Mountains. Made from stone, Machu Picchu had 200 buildings, including houses and temples.

Experts believe Machu Picchu was mainly used as a religious center, and normally had a population of about 300. In the winter months (June–August), visitors including royal family members came to Machu Picchu to escape the extreme cold of the capital, Cusco. At these times, the city was filled with over 1,000 people.

For nearly 100 years, Machu Picchu was a busy, peaceful city. Then, in 1532, the Inca people left the city. Machu Picchu, once a city of great strength, was left empty and forgotten for many centuries. Eventually the ancient site was found by an American explorer, ◄ **Hiram Bingham**, in 1911.

While Peru wants to encourage people from abroad to visit Machu Picchu, the country is also worried about negative influences of tourism. For this reason, only 500 people are allowed to climb the popular Inca Trail each day.

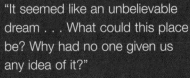

"It seemed like an unbelievable dream . . . What could this place be? Why had no one given us any idea of it?"

Hiram Bingham

Vocabulary Building 1

A. Word Link. The suffixes **–tion**, **–sion**, and **–ation** change verbs into nouns. Write the noun forms of the verbs below. Use your dictionary to help you. Then complete the information with the correct form of the words.

relate _relation_; organize _____; decide _____; define _____; explain _____;

invent _____; permit _____; populate _____; regulate _____; vacate _____

What's the smallest country in the world? One man says it's his country: the Principality of Sealand. It has a **1.** _____ of fewer than ten people!

Sealand is actually an old sea tower in the North Sea near England. A man named Paddy Roy Bates took the tower in 1967 in order to start a radio station. He formed a new "country" and **2.** _____ new money and a flag. But you can't just fly to Sealand. You need **3.** _____ to visit. Also, it isn't on any map. Part of the usual **4.** _____ of a country is that it must have land. Sealand doesn't. For this reason and others, it is not considered a real country.

Bates' son says there are advantages of having your own "country" like Sealand. It's a good place for a(n) **5.** _____—it's on the sea and is very peaceful. Also, there are very few **6.** _____; in fact, you can create all your own rules!

B. Word Partnership. Read the information and underline the phrases with **take**. Then use the correct form of the phrases to complete the sentences below.

TAKE A TRIP TO MOROCCO!

Visit Morocco and enjoy its lively marketplaces, ancient cities, and beautiful mountains and beaches!

In Morocco, most people take a break in the middle of the day for a long lunch. Remember to take advantage of this time and relax a bit yourself.

Two large music festivals take place in June: the World Music Festival and the Festival of World Sacred Music. Both concerts last for days, and artists from many different countries attend! Take our advice: see one of these concerts if you can.

▲ Take a camel ride in the Moroccan desert!

1. If you _____, you stop and relax for a short time.
2. If you _____, you travel somewhere.
3. If you _____ something, you use it well and it helps you.
4. If you _____ someone's _____, you follow their suggestion.
5. If something _____, it happens.

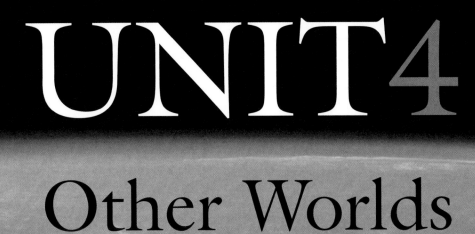

UNIT 4

Other Worlds

WARM UP

Discuss these questions with a partner.

1. Have you recently seen a movie or TV show about space? Describe it.
2. Do you think life exists on other planets? Why or why not?
3. Do you think governments should spend money on space travel and research? Why or why not?

▲ In 1984, Bruce McCandless II was the first person to walk freely in space.

4A

Making Contact

Before You Read

A. Labeling. Using the spaces below, label the numbered items in the pictures with the words in **blue**.

1 _____ **4** _____

2 _____ **5** _____

3 _____ **6** _____

The Hubble **Telescope** gets its name from **astronomer** Edwin Hubble (1889–1953). Since 1990, the Hubble Telescope has been sending images from space to Earth. It has sent pictures of the eight **planets** in our **solar system**. It has shown us how **stars** (like our sun) are born and die. It has also sent pictures of other planets and stars in our **galaxy** and other galaxies, such as NGC 4414, pictured above. With the Hubble Telescope, we have looked deep into space and have learned more about it and ourselves.

B. Predict. Read the first paragraph on the next page. Answer the questions below. Then read the whole passage to check your ideas.

1. What do Shostak and Barnett think?
   a. We might soon communicate with beings from space.
   b. We will probably never find intelligent life outside Earth.
   c. We have probably already contacted beings from space.
2. What is one possible reason for Shostak and Barnett's opinion?

Life Beyond Earth?

Is there intelligent life on other planets? For years, scientists said "no," or "we don't know." But today this is changing. Seth Shostak and Alexandra Barnett are astronomers. They believe intelligent life exists somewhere in the universe.[1] They also think we will soon **contact** these beings.[2]

Why do Shostak and Barnett think intelligent life exists on other planets? The first reason is time. Scientists believe the universe is about 12 billion years old. This is too long, say Shostak and Barnett, for only one planet in the **entire** universe to have intelligent life. The second reason is size—the universe is huge. **Tools** like the Hubble Telescope "have shown that there are at least 100 billion . . . galaxies," says Shostak. And our galaxy, the Milky Way, has at least 100 billion stars. Some planets **circling** these stars might be similar to Earth.

Looking for Intelligent Life

Until recently, it was difficult to **search** for signs of intelligent life in the universe. But now, **powerful** telescopes **allow** scientists to **identify** smaller planets—the size of Mars or Earth—in other solar systems. These planets might have intelligent life.

Making Contact

Have beings from space already visited Earth? Probably not, says Shostak. The **distance** between planets is too great. Despite this, intelligent beings might eventually contact us using other methods, such as radio signals.[3] In fact, they may be trying to communicate with us now, but we don't have the right tools to receive their **messages.** But this is changing, says Shostak. By 2025, we could make contact with other life forms in our universe.

Did You Know?

In 2007, scientists in Chile discovered the most Earth-like planet ever. Called Gliese 581c, it is about 20 light-years away from Earth.

◄ The Hubble Space Telescope has shown that there are billions of galaxies.

▼ A photo of a galaxy taken with the Hubble Telescope

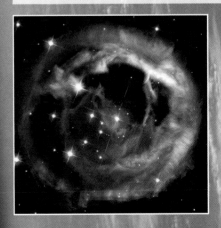

The **universe** is all of space—all stars, planets, and other objects.
A person or other living creature (for example, an animal) is a **being**.
A **radio signal** is a way of sending information using radio waves.

Reading Comprehension

A. Multiple Choice. Choose the best answer for each question.

Purpose **1.** What is the main purpose of this reading?
  a. to explain how life started on Earth
  b. to explain the beliefs of two scientists
  c. to show how telescopes work
  d. to describe what life on other planets might look like

Main Idea **2.** What would be a good title for the second paragraph?
  a. Earth: The Only Planet with Intelligent Life
  b. The Age and Size of the Universe
  c. Our Galaxy: The Milky Way
  d. Why Intelligent Life Might Exist

Detail **3.** Why was it harder to look for signs of intelligent life in the universe in the past?
  a. Planets used to be farther apart.
  b. We did not have the right tools.
  c. We could only see smaller planets from Earth.
  d. all of the above

Detail **4.** What kinds of planets are most likely to have intelligent life?
  a. smaller planets in our solar system
  b. smaller planets in other solar systems
  c. larger planets in our solar system
  d. larger planets in other solar systems

Reference **5.** In line 34, what does *life forms* refer to?
  a. messages   b. radio signals   c. intelligent beings   d. planets

B. Summary. Complete the diagram below with words from the reading.

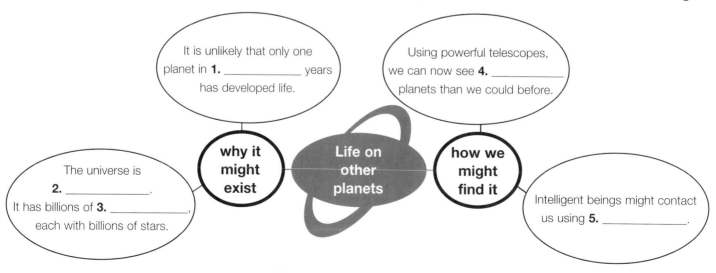

Vocabulary Practice

A. Completion. Complete the information with words from the box. One word is extra.

allow	powerful
identify	searching for
messages	tools

Does life exist on other planets? To answer this question, scientists are using different methods. Some use **1.** _____ radio telescopes. Using these, they hope to get **2.** _____ from intelligent life on faraway planets.

Other scientists are also **3.** _____ life in and outside our solar system. But these scientists aren't only looking for intelligent (human-like) life. They want to **4.** _____ any kind of living thing on other planets. To do this, these scientists use special **5.** _____ that test whether any kind of life exists on the planet.

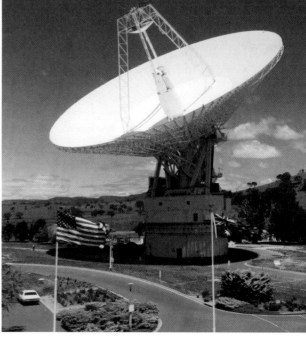

▲ This radio telescope in Canberra, Australia, is one of three that form NASA's Deep Space Network. The other two are in Madrid, Spain, and California, U.S.A.

B. Words in Context. Complete each sentence with the best answer.

1. We measure distance in _____.
   a. kilometers   b. kilograms

2. If exercise allows you to relax, it makes it _____ for you to relax.
   a. possible   b. difficult

3. If you contact someone, you communicate with him or her _____.
   a. in person   b. by phone, email, etc.

4. If you have lived in a place your entire life, you have lived there _____ of your life.
   a. some   b. all

5. The moon circles the Earth. This means the moon goes _____ the Earth.
   a. around   b. above

Word Partnership   Use *message* with:

(v.) **give someone** a message, **leave** a message, **take** a message, **get** a messsage, **send** a message;
(adj.) **clear** message, **important** message, **powerful** message, **strong** message.

4B

Living on the Red Planet

▲ This photo of the rocky surface of Mars was taken by the U.S. spaceship Viking 2 in 1976.

▲ In 1962 an Atlas rocket launched into space carrying John Glenn, the first American astronaut to orbit (travel around) the Earth.

Before You Read

A. Completion. Read the definitions. Complete the paragraph with the correct form of the words in **blue**.

astronaut: a person who travels into space
colony: a place where people with similar backgrounds live together
establish: to make or start something, e.g., a system or organization
◄ **rocket**: a vehicle used to travel to space

Robert Zubrin is a(n) **1.** _____ scientist; he designs spaceships. He thinks we should send **2.** _____ into space, but not just to visit. Zubrin wants to **3.** _____ a human **4.** _____ on the planet Mars. He wants to change the planet into a new place for humans to live.

B. Predict. Read the sentence below. Circle your answer and give reasons. Then read and compare your ideas with those in the passage.

Sending humans into space to live (is / is not) a good idea because . . .

_____

_____

_____

_____

COLONIES IN SPACE

1   Stephen Hawking, one of the world's most important scientists, believes that to **survive,** humans must move into space: "Once we **spread out** into space and
5   establish **independent** colonies, our future should be safe," he says.

Today, the United States, India, China, and Japan are all planning to send astronauts back to Earth's closest **neighbor**: the moon.
10 Each country wants to create space stations there between 2020 and 2030. These stations will prepare humans to visit and later live on Mars or other Earth-like planets.

Robert Zubrin, a rocket scientist, thinks humans should colonize space. He wants to start with Mars. Why? There are
15 several advantages: for one, sending people to the moon and Mars will allow us to learn a lot—for example, whether living on other planets is possible. Then, we can eventually create new human societies on other planets. In addition, the **advances** we make for space travel in the fields of science, technology,
20 **medicine**, and health can also **benefit** us here on Earth.

But not everyone thinks sending humans into space is a smart idea. Many say it's too expensive to send people, even on a short **journey**. And most space trips are not short. A one-way trip to Mars, for example, would take about six months. People
25 traveling this kind of distance face a number of health problems. Also, for many early space **settlers**, life would be extremely difficult. On the moon's **surface**, for example, the air and the sun's rays[1] are very dangerous. People would have to stay indoors most of the time.

30 Despite these concerns, sending people into space seems certain. In the future, we might see lunar[2] cities and maybe even new human cultures on other planets. First stop: the moon.

[1] The **sun's rays** are narrow beams of light from the sun.
[2] **Lunar** means "related to the moon."

"Once we spread out into space and establish independent colonies, our future should be safe."

–Stephen Hawking

Did You Know?
The meals astronauts eat in space include food like pasta and chocolate cake or, for Japanese astronauts, ramen noodles.

Reading Comprehension

A. Multiple Choice. Choose the best answer for each question.

Purpose **1.** What is the main purpose of this passage?
a. to give reasons for and against human space travel
b. to describe what life is like on the moon
c. to explain the history of space travel
d. to compare Mars and the moon

Detail **2.** Between 2020 and 2030, some countries plan to send astronauts to _____.
a. Mars   b. other Earth-like planets   c. the moon   d. another solar system

Detail **3.** Why are some countries creating space stations on the moon?
a. to learn more about human society on Earth
b. to lower Earth's population
c. to grow food for humans on Earth
d. to prepare humans to live on other planets

Inference **4.** Which statement would Stephen Hawking probably agree with?
a. Beings from other planets might colonize Earth.
b. Humans should stay on Earth, not move into space.
c. Humans should colonize other planets.
d. Human colonies won't be safe in space.

Vocabulary **5.** In line 18, we can change *In addition* to _____.
a. So   b. And   c. Or   d. However

B. For and Against. Complete the chart with information given in the reading.
Which side do you agree with?

Sending Humans into Space

Reasons for	Reasons against
1. We can learn if _____ on other planets is possible.	**1.** Space travel is very _____—it costs a lot of money.
2. We can create _____ on other planets.	**2.** Long trips in space can cause many _____ in humans.
3. The things we learn about _____, _____, health, and medicine can _____ humans on Earth.	**3.** Life on other planets would be very _____. People would have to _____ most of the time.

Vocabulary Practice

A. Completion. Complete the information with the correct form of words from the box. One word is extra.

benefit	settler
journey	surface
independent	survive

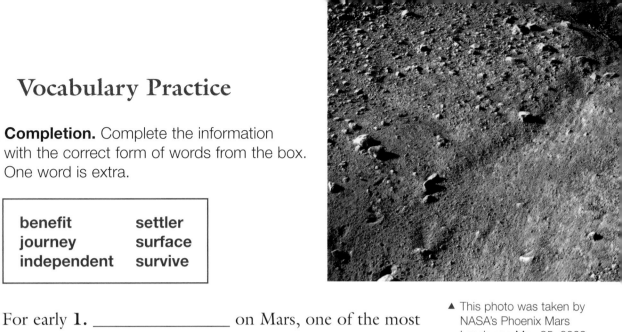

▲ This photo was taken by NASA's Phoenix Mars Lander on May 25, 2008. Scientists believe that water may still exist under the planet's surface.

For early **1.** _____ on Mars, one of the most difficult things at first would be finding water. On Earth, we use a lot of water every day.

On Mars, people would have to use much less—for example, by washing with a sponge and not taking a shower. Of course, we need water to **2.** _____. At first, we would have to bring it to Mars with us. But scientists think water existed on Mars in the past, and it may still be under the **3.** _____ of the planet. So, in time, as we change Mars, the planet might be able to have water again. This would then make us more **4.** _____ from Earth.

A trip to Mars would take at least a year—six months to get there and six months to return to Earth. This sounds like a long time, but think about it: people used to go on six-month **5.** _____ to Australia by ship all the time.

B. Words in Context. Complete each sentence with the best answer.

1. One of China's neighbors is _____.
   a. Chile   b. Mongolia
2. A person who studies medicine probably wants to be a(n) _____.
   a. doctor   b. astronaut
3. If a group of people spread out, they _____.
   a. come together in one place   b. move away from each other
4. If we make advances in science or technology, we _____ in those areas.
   a. do worse   b. improve
5. If something benefits you, it _____ you.
   a. helps   b. hurts

Word Link *in*, *im* = not: *independent, impolite, impossible*

The Moon

▲ A half moon is created as the moon circles the Earth.

A. Preview. Read the sentences. Then match each word in blue with a definition.

The Earth's atmosphere protects the planet from many things: the sun's rays, and even debris (like flying rocks) in space.

The Earth circles the sun. It takes about 365 days for it to complete one cycle around the sun.

1. broken pieces of something _____

2. the layer of air and other gases around the Earth _____

3. a series of repeating events _____

 B. Summarize. Watch the video, *The Moon.* Then complete the summary below using the correct form of words from the box. Two words are extra.

circle	entire	message	surface
contact	identify	neighbor	tool
distance	journey	powerful	

For centuries, people have studied the moon. In the past, some thought it was made of cheese. Others believed it was so
1. _____ it could change people into werewolves![1]
Today, we know a lot more about the moon:
- It's about one quarter the size of Earth.
- It's our nearest **2.** _____. The **3.** _____ to the moon is about 386,250 km (240,000 miles).
- It was formed about 4.6 billion years ago from rock and debris from the Earth.

In 1609, the scientist Galileo first looked at the moon with a(n)
4. _____ called a telescope. In 1969, astronauts Neil Armstrong and Buzz Aldrin made the first **5.** _____ from Earth. In a(n) **6.** _____ from the moon's
7. _____, Armstrong said, "That's one small step for man, one giant leap for mankind." The moon **8.** _____ the Earth, and it looks different in the sky at different times of the month. We call these different views the "phases of the moon."
It takes about 29 days for the moon to complete a(n)
9. _____ cycle from full to full.

[1] A **werewolf** is a being that is part human, part wolf.

C. Think About It.

1. How big is the moon? When and how did it form?

2. In the past, what were some beliefs about the moon? Are there any beliefs or stories about the moon in your country?

 To learn more about the moon and space travel, visit elt.heinle.com/explorer

UNIT 5 City Living

Discuss these questions with a partner.

1. Why do people live in cities?
2. What are some of the world's most important cities? Why are they important?
3. In your opinion, which is the best city in your country to live in? Which is the worst city to live in? Why?

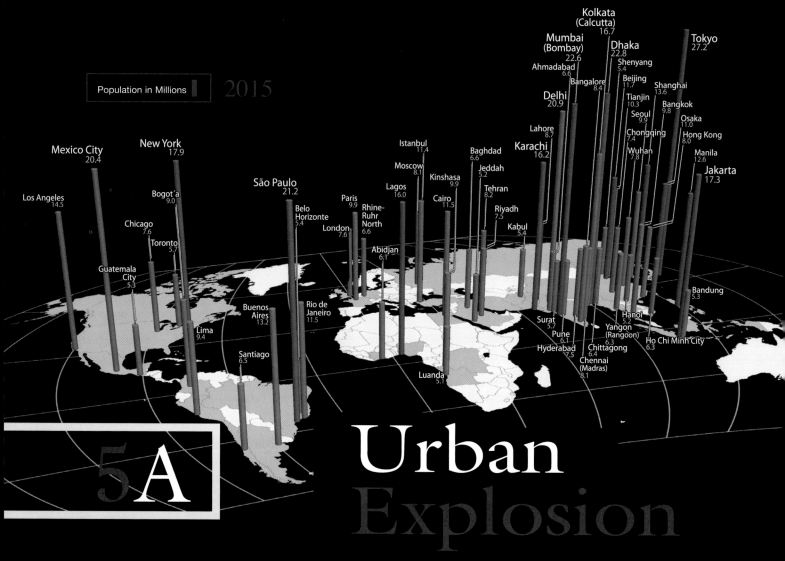

Population in Millions 2015

Mexico City 20.4 · New York 17.9 · Los Angeles 14.5 · Bogotá 9.0 · Chicago 7.6 · Toronto 5.7 · Guatemala City 5.3 · São Paulo 21.2 · Belo Horizonte 5.4 · London 7.6 · Paris 9.9 · Rhine-Ruhr North 6.6 · Buenos Aires 13.2 · Rio de Janeiro 11.5 · Lima 9.4 · Santiago 6.5 · Abidjan 6.1 · Lagos 16.0 · Luanda 5.1 · Istanbul 11.4 · Moscow 8.1 · Kinshasa 9.9 · Cairo 11.5 · Baghdad 6.6 · Jeddah 5.2 · Tehran 8.2 · Riyadh 7.5 · Kabul 5.4 · Kolkata (Calcutta) 16.7 · Mumbai (Bombay) 22.6 · Ahmadabad 6.6 · Bangalore 8.4 · Delhi 20.9 · Lahore 8.7 · Karachi 16.2 · Dhaka 22.8 · Shenyang 5.4 · Beijing 11.7 · Shanghai 13.6 · Tianjin 10.3 · Seoul 9.9 · Bangkok 9.8 · Chongqing 7.4 · Wuhan 7.8 · Tokyo 27.2 · Osaka 11.0 · Hong Kong 8.0 · Manila 12.6 · Jakarta 17.3 · Bandung 5.3 · Surat 5.7 · Pune 6.1 · Hyderabad 7.5 · Chittagong 6.3 · Chennai (Madras) 8.1 · Hanoi 5.2 · Yangon (Rangoon) 6.3 · Ho Chi Minh City 6.3

Urban Explosion

- In 1950, only one city in the world had more than ten million people—New York.
- By the year 2030, 60 percent of the world's population will live in cities.
- Many residents of large urban areas will face problems with housing, pollution (for example, of the air and water), and crime.

▲ In 2015, there will be 21 cities with a population of ten million or more.

Before You Read

A. Discussion. Study the map and the information. Then answer the questions below.

1. What was the first city to have a population of more than ten million?
2. In 2015, how many cities will have ten million people or more? Where will most of these cities be? What will be three of the largest cities?
3. What issues will people in these large cities face?

B. Predict. What can we do about the problems of city life? List two ideas. Then read the passage. Are any of your ideas mentioned?

City Challenges

Worldwide, cities gain a million people a week. This kind of **growth** brings problems, and today many of the world's largest cities face similar **challenges**: high housing costs, pollution, and crime (to name a few). What are some urban planners doing to **fix** these problems and improve people's lives?

▲ São Paulo, Brazil. Worldwide, cities grow by a million people a week.

Hyderabad, India (population: more than five million)

To improve residents' lives, Hyderabad is planting trees and parks. The city is even creating "greener" buildings that use less water and less **electricity** for power. Adding green to a city has a number of advantages. For example, trees **remove** pollution from the air and make it cleaner. In Hyderabad, streets were gray and **ugly** a few years ago. Today, they are filled with trees and flowers, making the city cleaner and more **colorful**. Green areas also give people places to relax or **exercise** and walk. A study in the U.S. showed something else interesting: the greener a neighborhood[1] is, the less crime there is against people and **property**—especially buildings and cars.

▲ In the city of Hyderabad, an old factory is now an urban park.

São Paulo, Brazil (population: more than eighteen million)

Many people work in the center of São Paulo, but they don't live there. They've spread out to neighborhoods outside the city, where housing is cheaper. Every day, these people travel into the city, and **traffic** is very heavy. Urban planners are using different strategies to address this issue. First, they are building better subways.[2] Another goal is to make it cheaper for people to live in the downtown area. Doing this will shorten the distance people travel for work and reduce traffic and pollution in the city.

[1] A **neighborhood** is one of the parts of a city where people live.
[2] A **subway** is an underground railroad. It is a type of public transportation in a city.

Reading Comprehension

A. Multiple Choice. Choose the best answer for each question.

Purpose **1.** What is the main purpose of this passage?
   a. to show how two cities are improving people's lives
   b. to describe the benefits of smaller cities
   c. to explain why more people are moving into cities
   d. to describe the life of an urban planner

Detail **2.** Which reason for making a city greener is NOT stated in the passage?
   a. It makes a city cleaner.
   b. It helps people work better.
   c. It lowers crime rates.
   d. It makes it easier to exercise.

Vocabulary **3.** In line 15, what does the word *greener* mean?
   a. more brightly colored
   b. better for the environment
   c. taller
   d. more full of trees

Detail **4.** According to the passage, what problem does São Paulo have?
   a. A lot of people don't have jobs.
   b. Too many people live in the city center.
   c. A lot of people are moving out of the city.
   d. Too many people drive into the city every day.

Reference **5.** In line 29, what does *there* refer to?
   a. Brazil   c. in a city
   b. outside São Paulo   d. central São Paulo

B. Classification. Match each answer (a–f) with the place it describes.

Hyderabad   São Paulo

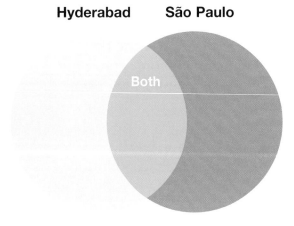

Both

a. is finding ways for people to live near their workplace
b. is adding trees and parks to the city
c. has less than ten million residents
d. is trying to reduce pollution
e. is making buildings that use less energy
f. is improving public transportation

Vocabulary Practice

A. Completion. Complete the information with the correct form of words from the box. One word is extra.

challenge	**colorful**	**exercise**
growth	**property**	**traffic**

Golden Gate Park, in San Francisco, California, is one of the largest urban parks in the United States. Today, over one million **1.** _____ flowers, trees, and other plants **2.** _____ in the park. But originally, most of the park was covered in sand. Creating a park in this environment was a big **3.** _____, but after a lot of work, the park was established in the 1870s. Today, Golden Gate Park is home to the oldest public Japanese garden in the U.S.A., as well as a number of art and science museums. People also visit the park to relax or **4.** _____. There are places to play basketball, soccer, golf, and many other sports. The park is also closed in many places to **5.** _____ so people can walk, cycle, or skate freely.

▲ Golden Gate Park contains the oldest public Japanese garden in the U.S.A.

B. Words in Context. Complete each sentence with the best answer.

1. If you fix something, you _____.
a. make it work again   b. break it

2. If something is ugly, it _____ nice to look at.
a. is   b. is not

3. If a city experiences growth, its population _____.
a. goes up   b. goes down

4. Without electricity, the _____ in your house will not work.
a. lights   b. water

5. If you remove a table from a room, you _____ the room.
a. bring it into   b. take it out of

Word Partnership   Use **traffic** with:

heavy traffic, **light** traffic, **oncoming** traffic, **stuck in** traffic.

5B City of the Future

▲ A foreign worker stacks fishing nets near the Burj Al Arab in Dubai, U.A.E.— one of the world's tallest hotels.

Dubai, UAE

Before You Read

A. Completion. Read the definitions. Complete the information with the correct form of the words in **blue**.

merchants: people who buy or sell things
port: an area of a city or town where ships stop
shopping mall: large, enclosed area with many shops
skyscrapers: very high buildings
trade: to buy and sell things

City Spotlight: Dubai

- For centuries, Dubai has been an important **1.** _____ city. Ships and **2.** _____ stopped here to **3.** _____ and do business.
- Dubai has some of the world's highest **4.** _____, including the Burj Al Arab and the Burj Dubai.
- Dubai is also home to some of the world's largest **5.** _____. Some have hundreds of stores, as well as theaters, restaurants, and sports centers.

B. Predict. Look quickly at the title and photo on the next page, and read the first sentence in each paragraph. Check (✔) the information you think you'll read about.

❑ religion in Dubai ❑ Dubai's population ❑ vacationing in Dubai
❑ building and growth in Dubai ❑ doing business in Dubai
❑ children in Dubai

DUBAI: THEN AND NOW

▲ Dubai is one of the world's fastest growing cities.

1 Dubai is like no other place on Earth. It is the world capital of living large—a city of big business, luxury[1] hotels, skyscrapers, and huge shopping malls. In the early 20th century, Dubai was a
5 **successful** trading port. People from all over the world stopped in Dubai to do business. But it was still a small city, and most people lived as fishermen, merchants, or by raising animals. Then in 1966, oil was discovered. In time, this
10 brought a lot of money into the region, and soon Dubai began to change.

Today Dubai is one of the world's most influential business centers. In fact, each year most of the city's **annual** earnings come from business, not oil.
15 The city is also a **global** trading port.

Recently Dubai has become a popular spot for **tourists**. People from abroad come to relax on its beaches, and every year, millions visit just to go shopping!

Dubai is also one of the world's fastest growing cities.
20 **Construction** is everywhere. Buildings (some of the tallest on Earth) are built in months. The city also has a number of man-made islands. One of these, the Palm Jumeirah, is **shaped** like a palm tree and is **particularly** beautiful.

The city is still an amazing mix of people from different
25 backgrounds. Individuals from 150 countries live and work in Dubai, and foreigners now outnumber[2] Dubai natives eight to one!

Many people **welcome** the city's growth. But an **increasing** number of Dubai natives have concerns[3] about the speed of
30 change. As Mohammad Al Abbar, a Dubai businessman, says, "We must always remember where we came from. Our **kids** must know we worked very, very hard to get where we are now, and there's a lot more work to do."

Did You Know?
Dubai has more shopping malls per person than any other city in the world.

---

[1] **Luxury** is very great comfort, especially relating to beautiful and expensive things.
[2] If one group of people **outnumbers** another, the first group has more people than the second group.
[3] A **concern** is a worry about a situation.

Reading Comprehension

A. Multiple Choice. Choose the best answer for each question.

Main Idea **1.** What is the main idea of this reading?
   a. Dubai is becoming an increasingly difficult place to live.
   b. Dubai is growing fast.
   c. Dubai is now very similar to other cities in the world.
   d. Dubai was a great city in the past, but this has changed.

Detail **2.** Before the mid-1960s, many people in Dubai lived _____.
   a. in skyscrapers   c. as fishermen and farmers
   b. on small islands   d. as oil workers

Detail **3.** Which sentence about Dubai is NOT true?
   a. Dubai now makes most of its money from selling oil.
   b. There are a lot of foreigners working in Dubai.
   c. Dubai gets many international visitors every year.
   d. Dubai has created several man-made islands.

Vocabulary **4.** In line 16, what does the word *spot* mean?
   a. a small, colorful circle (noun)   c. a mark on the skin (noun)
   b. a place, or destination (noun)   d. to see something (verb)

Inference **5.** In line 31, Mohammad Al Abbar says, "*We must always remember where we came from . . .*" What does this mean?
   a. We should always remember we are from Dubai.
   b. We should only think about the future—what to do next.
   c. We must always remember our past.
   d. We should always visit Dubai, even if we no longer live there.

B. Summary. Complete the information about Dubai with words from the reading.

Economy
• Today, the city earns most of its money from **1.** _____.

Growth
• Dubai is one of the **2.** _____-growing cities in the world.

Population
• People from over **3.** _____ nations live in Dubai.
  For every one Dubai native, there are **4.** _____ foreigners.

Things to do and see
• Relax on one of Dubai's **5.** _____ or go
  6. _____ in one of its many malls.

Vocabulary Practice

A. Matching. Read the information below. Then match each word in red with its definition.

The Palm Jumeirah was the first man-made island built in Dubai. Construction began in 2001 and was completed in 2006. Property here was particularly expensive, but this didn't stop people from buying all 4,000 homes on the island in 72 hours. The Palm also has a number of places for tourists to visit, including beaches, restaurants, shops, and parks.

There is also another group of islands, called "The World," being created in Dubai. These 300 islands are shaped like a map of the world. An entire island costs about 30 million U.S. dollars to buy, and sales have already been successful. The island of Ireland, for example, will become an Irish-themed vacation spot.

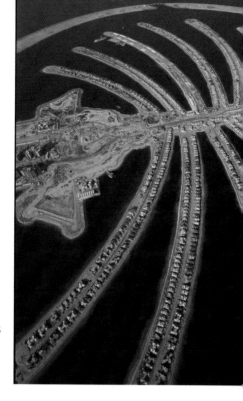

▲ The Palm Jumeirah was the first man-made island built in Dubai.

1. especially, very _____
2. doing well _____
3. building _____
4. in the form of _____
5. people who visit a place on vacation _____

B. Completion. Complete the sentences with the correct form of words from the box. One word is extra.

global	welcome	kid	increasing	particular	annual

1. In many cities, smoking isn't allowed in public places. Many people _____ this change.

2. Bullfighting . . . in Asia? Yes, the city of Jongdo in Korea has its _____ bullfighting festival every year in March.

3. A(n) _____ city (like Tokyo or London) is an important world center for business, culture, etc.

4. Las Vegas is now a child-friendly city, and many parents take their _____ there on vacation.

5. Every year, big cities around the world become _____ expensive to live in.

> **Word Link** We can add **–ful** to words to form adjectives (*colorful, successful, peaceful, powerful*). These adjectives mean "having a lot of something." For example, a *colorful* room has a lot of color.

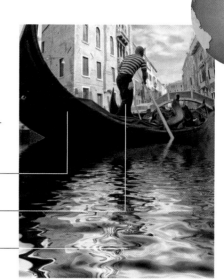

Venice, Italy

Living in Venice

A. Preview. Look at the photo and read the sentence. Label the photo with the words in blue.

A gondolier rows a gondola along a Venice canal. ▶

1. _____   _____

2. _____   _____

3. _____   _____

 B. Summarize. Watch the video, *Living in Venice*. Then complete the summary below using the correct form of words from the box. Three words are extra.

annual	increasing	property	tourist
challenge	kid	remove	welcome
colorful	particular	successful	

C. Think About It.

1. Why are some residents leaving Venice? Find the three reasons given in the passage.

2. Do people in your city face challenges like the ones mentioned in this unit? What can be done to help?

Venice: the Italian city of canals and gondolas. Today, this city has a problem. **1.** _____, many Venice natives— **2.** _____ the young—are leaving and moving to other places. Why? For one thing, **3.** _____ in Venice is very expensive. Parents want their **4.** _____ to stay, but for many young people, it's difficult to buy their own homes. Venice **5.** _____ visitors from all over the world—millions **6.** _____. At times, the large number of people in the streets can be very difficult for residents. Jobs are another problem. If one doesn't want to be a gondolier or do other work with **7.** _____, it can be hard to find a job.

Giovanni dal Missier lives in Venice. He wants to stay in his hometown. "I know that it's a very special gift . . . to live in a city [such] as Venice," he says. Despite all of the **8.** _____, Giovanni can't imagine living anywhere else.

 To learn more about cities around the world and the challenges they face, visit elt.heinle.com/explorer

UNIT 6

Clothing
and Fashion

Discuss these questions with a partner.

1. Do you know any famous fashion designers?

2. Where in your country or city can you see people wearing interesting clothes?

3. When was the last time you bought clothes or shoes? What did you buy?

▲ A woman with a silk wrap stands in
the Sierra Nevada Mountains, U.S.A.

6A From Sandal to Space Boot

Before You Read

A. Matching. Read the sentences. In the picture above, circle an example of each type of shoe.

- People often wear sneakers to play sports. In British English they are called "trainers."
- Some people think that high heels are hard to wear.
- Sandals are very common in hot countries.
- Boots are strong, heavy shoes that cover your foot and the lower part of your leg.

B. Predict. Look at the photos and captions on the next page. What do you think is special about these shoes? Read the passage to check your ideas.

More Than a Shoe?

1 **Stylish, futuristic**, different—these are some of the words used to describe Manolo Blahnik's and Dave Graziosi's shoes. What makes their shoes so special?

The Shoe Designer

5 Born to a Spanish mother and a Czech father, Manolo Blahnik grew up in the Canary Islands near north Africa. In his twenties, he moved to New York City and began to design shoes for women. Today, his high heels (often called "Manolos") are known around the world. "Women love my 10 shoes," says Blahnik. "Some never take them off."

Why are his shoes so popular? Yes, they're beautiful. On the other hand, his high heels aren't always particularly **comfortable**. They're also **costly**; prices **range** from hundreds to thousands of dollars. Maybe the best answer is this: each 15 **pair** of Manolos is a work of art—like a painting by Picasso.

But aren't they just shoes? "Yes, only shoes," says Blahnik. "But, if they bring a bit of happiness to someone, then, perhaps, they are something more than shoes."

The Shoe Engineer

20 At $30,000 a pair, moon boots aren't cheap. But to walk in space, you need high-tech shoes—like those designed by Dave Graziosi. He and his team are making space boots for NASA.[1] "We're planning for the moon and **beyond**," he says.

The latest space boot is the M2 Trekker. These boots are 25 smaller and **weigh** less than the ones Neil Armstrong[2] wore to the moon. In them, astronauts can walk comfortably on the moon's **rocky** surface. M2 Trekkers also protect astronauts' feet from extreme cold and **heat**. They can be worn in temperatures ranging from –212˚C (–350˚F) to +177˚C 30 (+350˚F). They are truly more than just a shoe!

[1] **NASA** (National Aeronautics and Space Administration) is a U.S. organization responsible for space travel.
[2] **Neil Armstrong** was the first astronaut to walk on the moon, in 1969.

"Women love my shoes. Some never take them off."
–MANOLO BLAHNIK

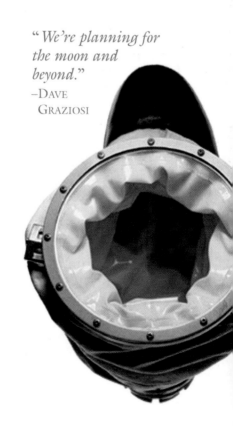

"We're planning for the moon and beyond."
–DAVE GRAZIOSI

Reading Comprehension

A. Multiple Choice. Choose the best answer for each question.

Gist **1.** Another title for this reading could be _____.
a. Shoes from Around the World
b. A History of the High Heel
c. Two Important Shoemakers
d. Shoes of the Future

Detail **2.** People often call Manolo Blahnik's shoes _____.
a. Canaries   b. Manolos   c. Picassos   d. Blahniks

Detail **3.** Which sentence about the M2 Trekkers is NOT true?
a. They can be worn in very hot or cold temperatures.
b. Neil Armstrong wore them on the moon.
c. They cost a lot of money.
d. Astronauts wear them.

Vocabulary **4.** In lines 11–12, we can change *On the other hand* to _____.
a. And   b. But   c. So   d. For

Reference **5.** In line 25, *the ones* means _____.
a. the space suits
b. the temperatures
c. the M2 Trekkers
d. the boots

B. Classification. Match each answer (a–e) with the person it describes.

Manolo Blahnik   Dave Graziosi

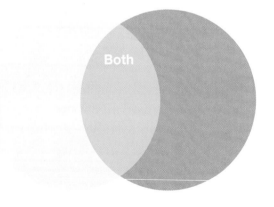

a. is designing a special boot
b. needs his shoes to be comfortable
c. says his shoes are like art
d. makes shoes that cost a lot of money
e. says shoes can make people happy

Vocabulary Practice

A. Matching. Match each word in red with a definition. One word is extra.

40,000 years ago: People in the Middle East and Europe start to wear sandals made of plants or leather. These shoes protect their feet from rocky ground, and cold and heat.

The 1700s: In Europe, shoes called *chopines* are popular with women. These shoes are stylish and beautiful, but they are not easy or comfortable to walk in. Some are extremely high: they range from 25–50 cm (10–20 inches) or more! Chopines are also costly. Only people with a lot of money can buy them.

1. very expensive _____
2. warmth, or a hot temperature _____
3. making one feel relaxed _____
4. well dressed and fashionable _____
5. to vary from one point to another _____

Ancient Shoes: This pair of sandals, now kept in a museum in Italy, dates from the 7th century B.C.

B. Completion. Complete the information using the correct form of words from the box. One word is extra.

beyond	futuristic	heat	pair	weigh

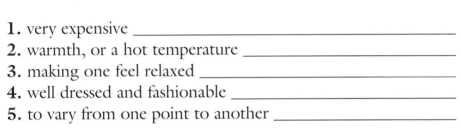

Fast feet: a modern sneaker

The 20th century and 1. _____: In the 1960s, University of Oregon coach Bill Bowerman helps to start a new sports-shoe company. Later, it becomes known as Nike, Inc.

Within a few years, sneakers are popular around the world. Today, designers are trying to create **2.** _____ of sneakers that are very light. Soon, we may see more **3.** _____ sport shoes that **4.** _____ almost nothing!

Word Link We can add **-y** to nouns to form adjectives, e.g., *rocky, dirty, sunny, smelly.*

6A From Sandal to Space Boot   **67**

6B The Silk Story

Before You Read

A. Completion. How much do you know about silk? Look at the pictures and captions and complete the paragraph.

Silk comes from **1.** _____, which aren't really worms. They are caterpillars. To become a moth, a silkworm first produces a long **2.** _____ from its mouth. It uses this to make a **3.** _____. We then **4.** _____ threads from the cocoons to make silk cloth.

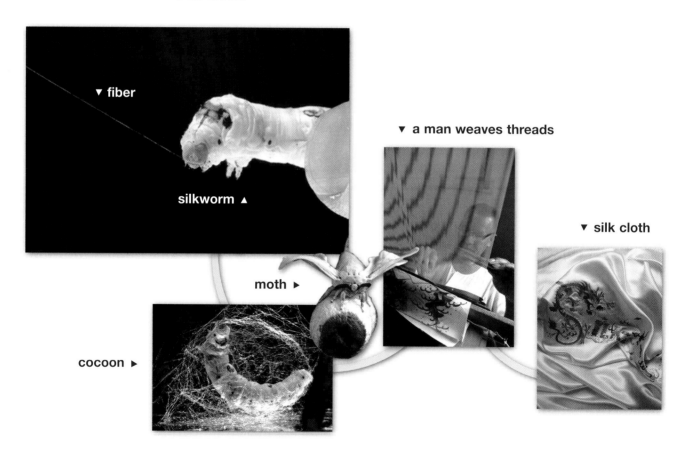

▼ fiber

silkworm ▲

▼ a man weaves threads

▼ silk cloth

moth ▶

cocoon ▶

B. Predict. Which country first used silk? Why do you think it has been popular for so many years? Read to check your answers.

The Miracle[1] of Silk

1   *Silk*. The word itself is beautiful. The story of silk starts in China over 4,000 years ago. One **legend** says a silkworm's cocoon fell into a woman's teacup. It then opened into a single, **unbroken** thread. This was an important **discovery**.
5   The Chinese learned they could use the cocoons to make **cloth** that was both beautiful to look at and soft to touch.

Making silk was a protected secret in China for many years. In other countries, silk was very **rare** and **valuable**. Often it was **worth** more than gold. Legend tells us that the secret
10   finally got out when a princess left China to go to India. In her hair, she secretly carried many silkworms.

By the year 1 A.D., silk was sold as far west as Rome, and all along the Silk Road, which connected China with places in the Middle East and the Mediterranean. Eventually, around
15   the year 300, silk also traveled from China to Japan. Centuries later, in 1522, the Spanish brought silkworms to Mexico.

▲ Silk shoes on sale at a market in China

Nowadays people around the world still make many beautiful
20   things from silk. But silk isn't only beautiful. It looks delicate,[2] but it's actually very strong. For example, it has been used to make bicycle tires. And some
25   doctors even use silk threads in hospital operations.[3] Silk is also lightweight and warm. This makes it great for clothes like winter **jackets**, pants, and boots.

30   All of this from a little **insect**— the silkworm. That is the miracle of silk.

▲ A silk robe

[1] A **miracle** is something that is very surprising or fortunate.
[2] If something is **delicate,** it is easy to break and needs to be handled carefully.
[3] During an **operation,** a surgeon cuts open a patient's body to remove, replace, or repair a diseased or damaged part.

Reading Comprehension

A. Multiple Choice. Choose the best answer for each question.

Gist **1.** This reading is mainly about _____.
a. how silk is made
b. different types of silk
c. the history of silk
d. a Chinese legend

Detail **2.** According to legend, how did people first learn about silk?
a. An Indian princess told people about it.
b. Someone found it on the Silk Road.
c. A man from Rome brought it to China.
d. A silkworm's cocoon fell into a woman's teacup.

Detail **3.** According to the passage, which sentence is NOT true?
a. Silk is very delicate.
b. A princess took silkworms to another country in her hair.
c. Sometimes doctors use silk in hospitals.
d. Silk can be comfortable to wear in cold weather.

Paraphrase **4.** In line 8, it says, *In other countries, silk was very rare and valuable. Often it was worth more than gold.* What does this mean?
a. You could only buy silk with gold.
b. Silk was very expensive.
c. Many people bought silk at that time.
d. In many countries, silk wasn't very popular.

Vocabulary **5.** In line 22, we can change the word *actually* to _____.
a. of course   b. luckily   c. only   d. in fact

B. Sequencing. Number the places, 1–5, in which people first used silk.

a. Rome   _____

b. China   _____

c. Mexico   _____

d. Japan   _____

e. India   _____

Vocabulary Practice

A. Words in Context. Complete each sentence with the best answer.

1. If something is valuable, it costs _____ money.
   a. very little   b. a lot of

2. A jacket is a type of short _____. You wear it to stay warm.
   a. dress   b. coat

3. A _____ is an insect that can fly.
   a. moth   b. bird

4. If something is unbroken, it is _____.
   a. in pieces   b. continuous and complete

B. Completion. Complete the biography of Marco Polo using words from the box. One word is extra.

| rare | cloth | valuable | nowadays | discovery | legends | worth |

▲ Marco Polo

Background
Marco Polo was from Venice, Italy. In 1271, at age 17, Marco went on a trip with his father and uncle to China. **1.** _____, people often travel to different places around the world. But in 1271, it was **2.** _____ for people from Europe to visit Asia.

Life in China
After three years, the Polos reached China. There are many **3.** _____ about Marco's life there. One story, probably true, is that while he was there he met and worked for the Mongol leader, Kublai Khan. While in China, Marco also made an interesting **4.** _____: in many places in China, people used paper money rather than gold to buy things. This was not common in Europe.

The Return Home
After 17 years in China, Marco and his family finally returned to Venice. The Polos brought with them silk **5.** _____, jewels, and spices, which were **6.** _____ a lot of money.

Word Link   The prefix **un-** before some words means "not" (*unbroken*, *unhappy*). For example, if something is *unbroken*, it is not broken.

Silk Weavers of Vietnam

Vong Nguyet, Vietnam

A. Preview. Look at the photo and read the information. Do you know anything else about how silk is made?

B. Summarize. Watch the video, *Silk Weavers of Vietnam*. Then complete the summary below using the correct form of words from the box. One word is extra.

▲ A female weaver uses a loom to turn silk thread into cloth.

cloth	heat	jacket	pair	rarely
comfortable	insect	nowadays	range	unbroken

We often think of silk as a soft material, used to make
1. _____ clothes. We **2.** _____ think of silk as something that comes from a moth! In the Vietnamese town of Vong Nguyet, people have made silk in the traditional way for 1,200 years—starting with the silkworm. How do they do it?

- For three weeks, they give silkworms leaves to eat every two to three hours.

- After three weeks, the silkworms make their cocoons. To do this, the **3.** _____ moves its head around in a circle. It produces a long, **4.** _____ silk fiber. This single fiber **5.** _____ from 400 to 600 meters long.

- Next, people **6.** _____ the cocoons in hot water. This frees the cocoons from the silkworms.

- People then take the cocoons and spin these together to make silk thread. **7.** _____, the people of Vong Nguyet still do a lot of this work by hand.

- When the silk thread is made, it goes to the town of Van Phuc. Here, looms weave the thread into silk **8.** _____. Eventually, this can be used to make different kinds of clothes, like **9.** _____, pants, and shirts.

C. Think About It.

1. Describe in your own words how silk is made in Vong Nguyet.

2. Is your city or country known for a special kind of clothing or clothing tradition?

To learn more about clothing and fashion, visit elt.heinle.com/explorer

A. Crossword. Use the definitions below to complete the missing words.

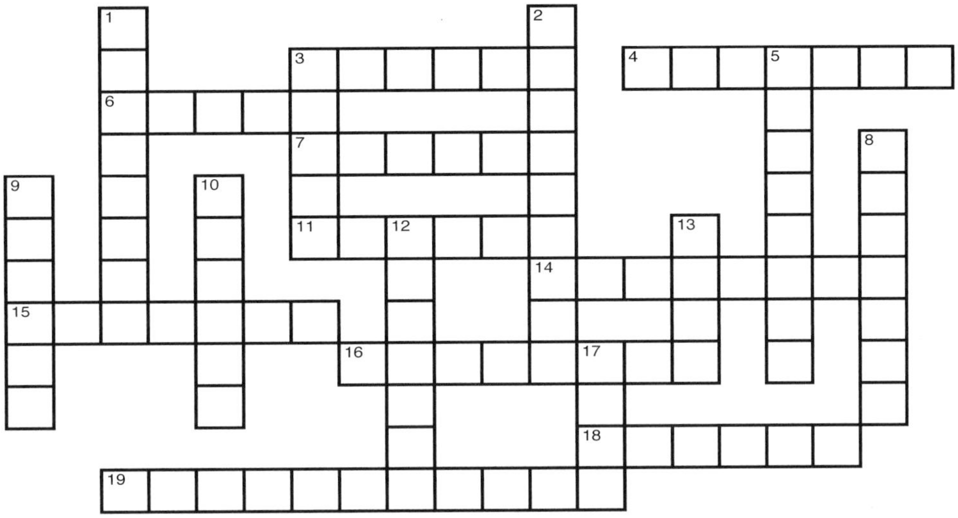

Across

3. to look for something
4. to stay alive
6. to measure how heavy something is
7. once every year
11. all; the whole of (something)
14. a person who lives near you
15. to greet someone when they arrive
16. something you own, such as a house
18. to take something away from a place
19. making you feel relaxed

Down

1. very strong
2. something difficult
3. to form something in a certain way
5. very important or worth a lot of money
8. a trip
9. an increase in size
10. on the far side of (something)
12. a person who visits a place on vacation
13. unattractive to look at
17. not common

B. Notes Completion. Scan the information on pages 74–75 to complete the notes.

Field Notes

Site: Gyeongju Historic Areas   **Location:** Korea

Information:

- Korean capital city was ruled by the _____
  Dynasty for nearly _____ years
- Queen Seondeok built the "Tower of the _____ and
  _____" in the _____ century
- Other sites include Mt. Namsan, and Silla _____ in town center
- About _____ tourists now visit every year

Site: Historic Monuments of Ancient Kyoto   **Location:** Japan

Information:

- Japan's capital for over _____ years
- _____ historic properties are now World Heritage Sites
- Ryoanji Temple is famous for its garden with 15 _____
- Visit _____ to see a geisha performance

Site:	**Gyeongju Historic Areas**
Location:	**Korea**
Category:	**Cultural**
Status:	**World Heritage Site since 2000**

Kyoto, Japan

Gyeongju, Korea

In the eighth century, one million Koreans lived in Gyeongju (Kyongju), a lively coastal city filled with Buddhist art and temples. For nearly 300 years the entire country was united, with Gyeongju as its capital, under the rule of the powerful Silla Dynasty. Nowadays, a population of only 150,000 Koreans calls Gyeongju home. However, over five million tourists come annually to see the place where Korea was born.

Must See Sights In Gyeongju

Silla Tombs In the center of Gyeongju, a city park hides more than 20 stone tombs. In one tomb removed in 1973, 11,500 items of valuable cultural and historical worth were discovered.

Mt. Namsan Only a short distance from Gyeongju, this rocky mountain has many temples and rock reliefs. Hundreds of items of artistic and cultural importance can be viewed here.

Cheomseongdae or "Tower of the Moon ▶ and Stars" was built by Queen Seondeok, one of three female rulers in the Silla Dynasty. Queen Seondeok was known especially for her intelligence. In the seventh century, she constructed this bottle-shaped tower as a tool for studying the night sky.

"My former home, dreaming of return, springtime beneath the sun . . . "
Ch'oe Chi'won, Silla poet

Glossary

capital: the ruling city of a country
dynasty: a series of rulers from the same family
shrine: a religious holy place
tomb: a place where a body is buried, often made of stone

In Japan, Korea's neighbor across the sea, the city of Kyoto became the country's capital at the end of the 8th century. During the next 1,000 years, over 1,600 religious buildings were constructed, including temples, shrines, and gardens. In 1994, 17 properties were identified as UNESCO World Heritage Sites, all still in extremely good condition. Although a modern city with crowds and heavy traffic, today's Kyoto is still heavily influenced by tradition. Everything here, from food to dance, is a stylish form of art.

Site: **Historic Monuments of Ancient Kyoto**

Location: **Japan**

Category: **Cultural**

Status: **World Heritage Site since 1994**

Kyoto, Japan
Gyeongju, Korea

► A view of modern-day Kyoto from the 8th century Toji temple

"Though the body moves, the soul may stay behind."

Murasaki Shikubu, Japanese poet and writer

Must See Sights In Kyoto

Gion is most famous as the home of one of Japan's oldest and most popular forms of performance art: geisha. For centuries, geisha women have been a familiar sight in Kyoto, entertaining audiences with their gentle songs and dances in theaters and teahouses around Gion.

Ryoanji Temple 15 rocks have been carefully placed around this Buddhist dry garden—yet from any viewpoint, only 14 rocks can be seen. Some tourists come here just to relax; others try to look beyond the surface in search of a deeper meaning. ▼

☐ Vocabulary Building 2

A. Word Link. The prefixes **in-**, **im-**, and **un-** are used to mean *not*. Use *in-*, *im-*, or *un-* to write the opposites of the adjectives below. Use your dictionary to help you. Then complete the sentences below with the correct form of the words.

important _____; **comfortable** _____; **polite** _____; **correct** _____;

successful _____; **perfect** _____; **direct** _____; **experienced** _____; **likely** _____

1. An astronaut's space suit is often quite heavy and _____ to wear.

2. Referring to women as "females" can often sound _____.

3. For years, scientists have tried to make contact with beings from space, but up to now, they have been _____.

4. _____ people cannot visit the international space station; "space tourists" must train for months to prepare for their trip.

5. Today, calling Pluto a planet would be _____. It is not a planet like Earth or Mars.

B. Word Partnership. Read the information and underline the phrases with **make**. Then use the correct form of the phrases to complete the sentences below.

World leaders are planning to return to the moon in the near future. Two companies—the Internet company Google and the X Prize Foundation, an organization that gives money for inventions—have also made a decision to support space travel. Together, they will give 30 million U.S. dollars to the first members of the public who send a rover[1] to the moon and send video back to Earth over the Internet. As well as making a lot of money, the winners will also make history—by being the first "regular people" to explore space.

Does it make sense for regular people to explore space? Yes, say the X Prize supporters. In the 1400s, they say, Christopher Columbus made a deal with Spain's leaders. They gave Columbus money to explore the world. In return, they learned about a whole new part of the world. Today's lunar explorers are similar. Who knows what they will discover?

[1] a **rover** is a vehicle that can travel on rough rocky ground.

1. If you _____, you can buy more things.
2. If you _____, you choose to do something.
3. If you _____, you are the first person ever to do something important.
4. If something _____, it is practical or the right thing to do.
5. If you _____ with someone, you both promise to do something for the other person.

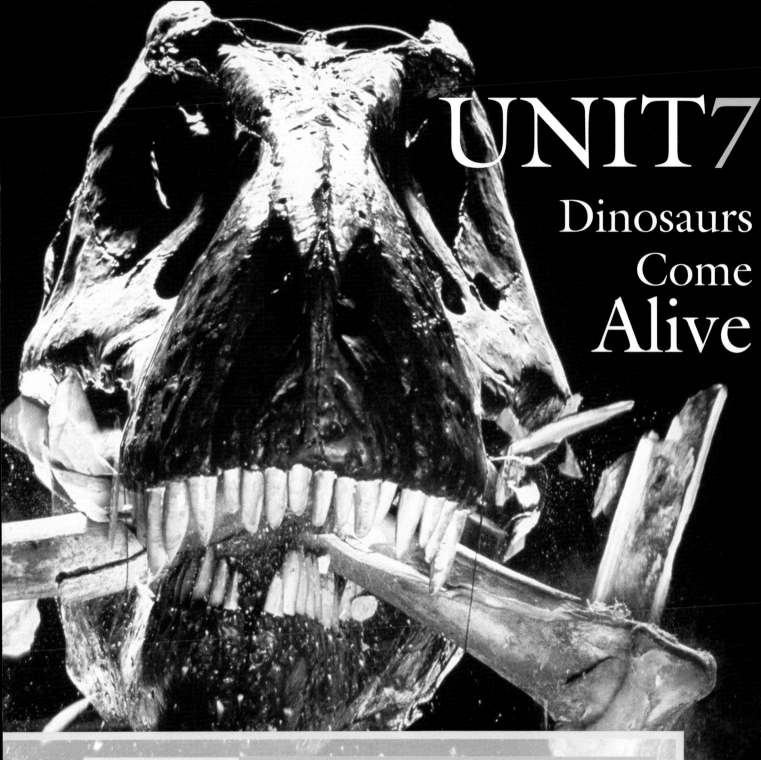

UNIT7
Dinosaurs
Come
Alive

WARM UP

Discuss these questions with a partner.

1. What do you know about dinosaurs?
2. Have you ever seen a movie about dinosaurs? Describe it.
3. Why do you think people are interested in dinosaurs?

▲ A model of a *Tyrannosaurus rex*
shows how it ate its prey.

Prehistoric Timeline

Masiakasaurus

When:
65–70 million years ago

Where:
Madagascar, Africa

With its long, sharp teeth, *Masiakasaurus* was a powerful **predator**.

Before You Read

A. Discussion. Read the timeline, paying attention to the words in **blue**. Then answer the questions below.

The Triassic Period	The Jurassic Period	The Cretaceous Period	
(248) million years ago	(206) million years ago	(144) million years ago	(65) million years ago

248 million years ago: Earth's warm and dry temperatures are perfect for **reptiles**. These animals become common on Earth, and some grow to huge sizes.

240 million years ago: The oldest-known dinosaur, discovered by **paleontologists** in Madagascar, dates back to this time.

65 million years ago: Dinosaurs become **extinct**.

1. What kind of animals were dinosaurs?
2. When did dinosaurs die out completely?
3. What is a *paleontologist*?
4. What does a *predator* eat?

B. Predict. Read the four questions in the paragraph headings on the next page and answer **Yes** or **No**. Then read the passage to check your answers.

DINOSAURS: FACT & FICTION

1 You learned about dinosaurs in school. Maybe you have
seen them in a **museum**. But how much do you really
know about these animals?

Were dinosaurs just big reptiles?

5 For years, scientists thought dinosaurs were big, dumb,[1]
and cold-blooded—in other words, just **giant** reptiles.
Some dinosaurs *were* huge. But many were about the size
of modern-day birds or dogs. Were dinosaurs warm- or
cold-blooded? Paleontologists are not sure. But they believe
10 some were intelligent. Of course, no dinosaur was as smart
as a human or even a monkey. However, some smaller
dinosaurs—like the two-meter (six-foot) *Troodon*—
had fairly large brains.

▲ A scientist with a
mechanical *Troodon*

▼ *Tyrannosaurus rex*

Was *Tyrannosaurus rex* a powerful predator?

15 Some scientists think the **opposite** is true. In the
movies, *T. rex* is often a **speedy** giant, but in fact, this
dinosaur could not run very fast. **Physically**, it was too
large. **In reality**, *T. rex* probably moved as fast as an
elephant. Also, *T. rex* had very small arms. Without strong legs
20 or arms, this dinosaur probably wasn't a powerful
hunter. It may have been a scavenger instead, only eating
animals that were already dead.

Did an asteroid kill the dinosaurs?

An asteroid hit Mexico's Yucatán Peninsula about 65 million
25 years ago. It created a 180-kilometer (110-mile) wide crater
called *Chicxulub*. Many believe this asteroid caused the
extinction of the dinosaurs. But even before this, dinosaurs were
already dying out[2] around the world, for many reasons. At the
end of the Cretaceous period, for example, the global **climate**
30 was changing: the Earth's temperature was getting colder.

Are all dinosaurs now extinct?[2]

Dinosaurs **completely** disappeared about 65 million years ago.
However, scientists believe modern-day birds are descendants[3]
of certain dinosaurs. If this is true, then dinosaurs' **relatives**
35 are still walking—and flying—among us!

▲ A crater caused by an
asteroid hitting the Earth
in Australia

[1] If something is **dumb**, it is not smart.
[2] If something **dies out** or becomes **extinct**, it becomes less common and finally disappears.
[3] Your **descendants** are people in later generations who are related to you.

Reading Comprehension

A. Multiple Choice. Choose the best answer for each question.

Gist **1.** Another title for this reading could be _____.
    a. What Really Killed the Dinosaurs?
    b. The Truth about Dinosaurs
    c. Dinosaurs Discovered in Mexico
    d. Our Favorite Dinosaurs

Inference **2.** Which statement about the *Troodon* is probably true?
    a. It was smarter than a monkey.
    b. It was warm-blooded.
    c. It was a huge animal.
    d. It was quite intelligent.

Vocabulary **3.** Some paleontologists think *T. rex* was a *scavenger* (line 21).
    What does this mean?
    a. It had small arms.
    b. It was a powerful killer.
    c. It was similar to an elephant.
    d. It ate animals that were already dead.

Detail **4.** What is *Chicxulub*?
    a. a huge hole caused by an asteroid
    b. a type of dinosaur found in Mexico
    c. a time in dinosaur history
    d. an animal *T. rex* ate

Detail **5.** At the end of the Cretaceous period _____.
    a. some dinosaurs started to fly
    b. humans appeared on Earth
    c. the Earth's temperature was changing
    d. dinosaur numbers were increasing in Mexico

B. True or False. Read the sentences below and circle **T** (true), **F** (false), or **NG** (not given in the passage).

1.	Some dinosaurs were small.	**T**	**F**	**NG**
2.	All dinosaurs had small brains.	**T**	**F**	**NG**
3.	Paleontologists agree that dinosaurs were cold-blooded.	**T**	**F**	**NG**
4.	*T. rex* was a fast runner.	**T**	**F**	**NG**
5.	A young *T. rex* probably had feathers like a bird.	**T**	**F**	**NG**
6.	Some scientists believe that modern-day birds are related to dinosaurs.	**T**	**F**	**NG**

Vocabulary Practice

A. Matching. Read the information and match each word in red with its definition.

▲ An ancient sea reptile fossil in Beijing, China

T. rex and other giant land dinosaurs went extinct about 65 million years ago. Today, you only see these animals in a **museum**. But what about the **huge** animals that lived in the seas millions of years ago? Are they still alive—living in the world's lakes and oceans?

For centuries, stories about sea monsters have existed in many countries. One of the most famous is Scotland's Loch Ness Monster (often called "Nessie"). In reality, these legendary animals are similar to **actual** reptiles that lived in the world's seas 65–250 million years ago. For example, Nessie is **physically** similar to a type of plesiosaur— a sea reptile with a very long neck. But is Nessie really an ancient sea monster, still alive in a lake in Scotland? Probably not. Plesiosaurs (like the dinosaurs) died out **completely** about 65 million years ago.

1. actually, in fact _____
2. huge, very large _____
3. totally _____
4. related to the body _____
5. a building where historical items are kept for people to see _____

B. Completion. Complete the information using words from the box. One word is extra.

climate	hunter	opposite	relative	speedy

The ancient sea monster *Dakosaurus* (nicknamed "Godzilla") is a(n) **1.** _____ of modern-day crocodiles. This South American sea reptile was a(n) **2.** _____ swimmer and a powerful **3.** _____.

Sea reptiles like *Dakosaurus* were top predators. And some, like *Tylosaurus*, even attacked sharks. But in the end, sharks were the real survivors. Today, they are still alive, but changes in the Earth's **4.** _____ caused the larger sea reptiles to become extinct.

> **Word Link**
>
> We can add **–er** or **–or** to words to form nouns. These nouns often describe a person who does a certain action or job, for example, *hunter* or *inventor*.

▲ *Epidendrosaurus*
(160 million years ago).
Discovered in China.

▲ *Carnotaurus*
(67–82 million years ago).
Discovered in Argentina.

7B Strange Dinosaurs

Before You Read

A. **Completion.** Read the definitions. Then complete the paragraph below with the correct form of the words in **blue**. What is unusual about the dinosaurs pictured above?

claws: the long, sharp nails on the toes of some animals
fossils: the bones or remains of an animal or plant
horns: the hard things on top of an animal's head
unearth: to take something out of the ground; to discover something

Dinosaurs looked strange. Some had **1.** _____ on their heads. Others had **2.** _____ like giant knives. Several (like the *Carnotaurus*) had huge bodies but very small arms. Paleontologists continue to **3.** _____ different dinosaurs all over the world. Each time, these dinosaur **4.** _____ are stranger than before. Today, scientists are asking: what was the purpose of these unusual features—the horns, the strange claws, the small arms? And what can they tell us about dinosaurs?

B. **Predict.** Look at the pictures on the next page. What do you think is unusual about this dinosaur? Read the passage to check your ideas.

MYSTERY OF THE TERRIBLE HAND

1 **Name:** Deinocheirus
Lived when: 70 million years ago
Discovered where: Mongolia

Whose arms are these? Paleontologists have **sought**
5 an answer to this question for almost forty years.
In the 1960s, paleontologists unearthed a pair
of giant arms in Mongolia. The **length** of
each, when fully **extended**, was 2.4 meters
(eight feet). The claws were 26 centimeters
10 (ten inches) long. Paleontologists called the
animal *Deinocheirus* (meaning "**terrible** hand").

So what did this animal look like? Paleontologists
aren't sure. Many times, scientists have **examined** the area
where they found the arms. But since the original discovery,
15 they have unearthed only a few other bones of this dinosaur.

▲ *Deinocheirus:* the body
is a mystery.

Despite this, scientists have some ideas about *Deinocheirus's*
appearance. Physically, this animal's arms and hands are
similar to *ornithomimids*—a type of dinosaur that looked like a
modern-day ostrich[1] and used its arms for catching food. But
20 when paleontologists use the size of *Deinocheirus's* arms to try
to **estimate** the size of its body, it seems to have been a huge
animal—almost 12 meters (40 feet) long. This is almost as big
as a *T. rex*!

Other scientists have a different **opinion**. They think
25 *Deinocheirus* was a smaller dinosaur with extremely long arms.
But why would a little animal need limbs[2] so long? To climb
trees or to hunt for food, perhaps? "The body is a **mystery**,"
says Thomas Holtz, a paleontologist at the University of
Maryland in the U.S. "It might not be an ornithomimid at all.
30 But then what is it?" Until paleontologists find new fossil
evidence, this question remains **unanswered**.

▲ Was *Deinocheirus*
a huge animal?

---

[1] An **ostrich** is a very large bird that cannot fly.
[2] Your **limbs** are your arms and legs.

Reading Comprehension

A. Multiple Choice. Choose the best answer for each question.

Purpose   **1.** What is the main purpose of the reading?
- a. to explain how paleontologists find dinosaur fossils
- b. to compare *T. rex* and *Deinocheirus*
- c. to talk about different dinosaur discoveries in Mongolia
- d. to describe an unusual type of dinosaur

Detail   **2.** *Deinocheirus* _____.
- a. had very short fingers on its hand
- b. had very long arms
- c. had very few bones in its body
- d. could fly like a bird

Detail   **3.** Which modern-day animal is *Deinocheirus* most similar to?
- a. a monkey   b. a horse   c. an ostrich   d. a lizard

Vocabulary   **4.** What does the word *evidence* mean in line 31?
- a. information   b. questions   c. mysteries   d. beliefs

Inference   **5.** Which statement would Thomas Holtz probably agree with?
- a. *Deinocheirus* was a huge and dangerous predator.
- b. *T. rex* was a relative of *Deinocheirus*.
- c. *Deinocheirus* was a small dinosaur with very long arms.
- d. We don't know for sure what *Deinocheirus* looked like.

B. Completion. Complete the paleontologist's notes with information from the reading.

Name: Deinocheirus (meaning: 1. _____)

Discovered when: 2. _____ Discovered where: 3. _____

Today, paleontologists have only the dinosaur's 4. _____.
Each was about 5. _____ long.

Two ideas about what this dinosaur looked like:
Maybe it was a 6. _____ animal
(about the same size as 7. _____)

Maybe it was a 8. _____ animal with really
9. _____. The dinosaur probably used these to
10. _____ or _____.

Vocabulary Practice

A. Completion. Complete the information using the correct form of words from the box. One word is extra.

| appearance estimate examine extend length seek |

The largest ever flying animal lived 85 million years ago. It was a type of pterosaur (or "flying reptile") called *Quetzalcoatlus*. When this animal's wings were **1.**_____, each was about 12 meters (40 feet) in **2.** _____—the size of some airplanes! But did pterosaurs come from a smaller animal? And how did pterosaurs learn to fly? For years, paleontologists have **3.** _____ answers to these questions and others.

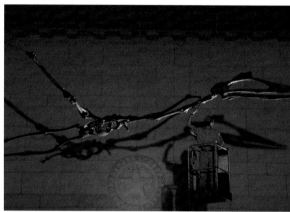

▲ A paleontologist with the bones of *Quetzalcoatlus* in Texas Memorial Museum, U.S.A.

Recently, one of the smallest pterosaurs was discovered in China by a team of Chinese and Brazilian paleontologists. In **4.** _____, the tiny pterosaur (called *N. crypticus*) was a small, toothless reptile with feet similar to a bird's. Scientists **5.** _____ that about 120 million years ago, this animal lived in trees in China. The world's huge pterosaurs, they believe, were descendents of *N. crypticus*.

B. Words in Context. Complete each sentence with the best answer.

1. If you examine something, you _____.
   a. look at it quickly   b. study it closely

2. A mystery is something you _____ explain.
   a. can   b. cannot

3. An example of an opinion is _____.
   a. "Dinosaurs are very interesting animals."
   b. "Dinosaurs were reptiles."

4. If something is terrible, it makes you feel _____.
   a. afraid   b. relaxed

5. An unanswered question _____ been explained.
   a. has   b. hasn't

Word **Partnership**

Use *opinion* with:
different opinion, **expert** opinion,
honest opinion, **popular** opinion,
ask an opinion, **give** an opinion,
share an opinion.

Dinosaur Discovery

Sabinas, Mexico

A. Preview. Label the picture using the words in the box. Use a dictionary to help you.

neck	tail	rib	back bone	vertebra

1. _____

2. _____

3. _____

4. _____

5. _____

B. Summarize. Watch the video, *Dinosaur Discovery*. Then complete the summary below using the correct form of words from the box. Three words are extra.

climate	completely	examine	extend
giant	hunt	length	museum
opinion	opposite	relative	seek

Near the town of Sabinas in Mexico, scientists have discovered a(n) **1.** _____ dinosaur. The animal is about 15 meters (50 feet) in **2.** _____ and 4.5 meters (15 feet) tall. Why is this discovery important? It shows that Sabinas was once a jungle. Sabinas is now a desert. The **3.** _____ in this area has changed **4.** _____. Why? Scientists are **5.** _____ an answer to this question.

An engineer first discovered some of the dinosaur's bones. He was **6.** _____ the land for a construction project. Later, children found more bones. Now paleontologists are **7.** _____ for the rest of the fossils. In their **8.** _____, this might be the most complete dinosaur skeleton in Latin America. The mayor of Sabinas wants to keep the dinosaur's fossils in a(n) **9.** _____ for people to see. He also wants paleontologists around the world to know about "Sabinasaurio" and other dinosaur discoveries in the area.

C. Think About It.

1. How do you think the mayor of Sabinas feels about the discovery?

2. Which of the dinosaur discoveries in this unit do you think is most interesting? Why?

 To learn more about dinosaur discoveries, visit elt.heinle.com/explorer

Stories and Storytellers

Discuss these questions with a partner.

1. What is one of your favorite books or stories? Why do you like it?
2. Describe a popular author. What has he or she written? Why do you think he/she is popular?
3. Can you name a legend or traditional story from your country?

▲ A boy and girl walk through a forest in Germany.
Many medieval fairy tales take place in forests.

8A Collectors of Tales

▲ **Hansel and Gretel**
In this story, a brother and sister get lost in a forest. There, they meet a bad witch who tries to eat them.

▲ **Little Red Riding Hood**
In this story, a young girl walks to her grandmother's house. On the way, she meets a wolf that wants to eat her.

Before You Read

A. Discussion. Look at the books above. Do you know these stories? Are there similar stories in your country?

B. Predict. Look at the title, headings, pictures, and captions on the next page, and answer the questions below. Then read the passage to check.

1. Where were the men from?
2. When did they write?
3. Who were their stories for?

The Brothers Grimm

1 Long before J.K. Rowling,[1] there were Jacob and Wilhelm Grimm—two young men from Germany who loved a good story. The Grimm brothers never expected to be storytellers for children. But today,
5 their fairy tales are read and loved in over 160 languages.

▲ The Brothers Grimm: Jacob (right) and Wilhelm

Once Upon a Time

Jacob and Wilhelm were introduced to folktales—traditional stories people **memorized** and told again
10 and again—as university students. The brothers loved these stories of adventure and magic. Soon they began to **collect** traditional folktales from storytellers in Germany. Many of these tales were similar to stories told in France, Italy, Japan, and other countries. Between
15 1812 and 1814, the Grimm brothers published two books. These included stories like *Hansel and Gretel* and *Little Red Riding Hood*.

Grimms' tales **reflected** traditional life and beliefs in Germany. For example, forests are common in Germany, and this image
20 appears often in the Grimms' stories. For medieval[2] Germans, the forest was a dangerous place. In Grimms' fairy tales, witches, talking animals, and other **magical** beings live in the forest. People's lives change forever when they visit this place.

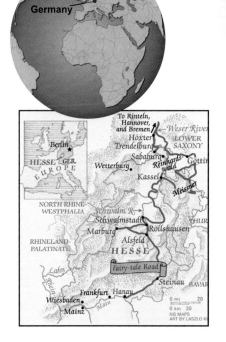

Children's Stories?

25 **Although** Grimms' fairy tales are now considered children's stories, the brothers first wrote them **primarily** for adults. Many of the early tales were dark and a little **scary**.

Later, the brothers changed the **text** of some of the original stories. They "**softened**" many of the tales and also
30 added drawings. This made them more **appropriate** for children. Like the early tales, though, each of today's stories still has a moral: work hard, be good, and listen to your parents.

▲ Along Germany's "Fairy Tale Road" tourists can travel past dark forests and old villages. The 550-km road begins in the town of Hanau, the Grimm brothers' birthplace.

[1] **J.K. Rowling** wrote the *Harry Potter* books.
[2] The **medieval** period is a time in European history from A.D. 476 to about A.D. 1500.

Reading Comprehension

A. Multiple Choice. Choose the best answer for each question.

Purpose
1. What is the main purpose of the reading?
   a. to describe the Grimm brothers and their stories
   b. to explain why storytelling is important in Germany
   c. to examine two of the Grimms' fairy tales
   d. to compare the Grimms' stories to modern children's stories

Detail
2. The Grimm brothers _____.
   a. invented the fairy tales in their books
   b. always wanted to write children's stories
   c. became interested in folktales as students
   d. were actually French but moved to Germany

Reference
3. In line 26, what does *them* refer to?
   a. the Grimm brothers   c. the fairy tales
   b. the children   d. the adults

Detail
4. Which sentence about the Grimms' later fairy tales is true?
   a. They were for adults.   c. Children didn't like them.
   b. They had pictures.   d. They were darker.

Vocabulary
5. In line 32, what does *moral* mean?
   a. interest   b. text   c. story   d. message

B. Summary. Complete the information with words from the reading.

Vocabulary Practice

A. Completion. Complete the information with the correct form of words from the box. Two words are extra.

Viena Karelia, Finland

although	**appropriate**	**collection**	**magical**
memorize	**primarily**	**reflect**	**scary**
soften	**text**		

In Finland, there once was a region known as Viena Karelia. The people here were great storytellers and had many folktales and legends. The most famous is the *Kalevala*. This is a(n) **1.** _____ of several poems that forms one long story. The *Kalevala* tells tales of **2.** _____ beings and **3.** _____ monsters.

For centuries, storytellers, called *rune singers*, have learned and spoken the *Kalevala* from memory. Today, Jussi Huovinen is Finland's last great rune singer. When he dies, the ancient line of rune singers will end, **4.** _____ because no one has **5.** _____ the entire *Kalevala*.

But there is good news. **6.** _____ Jussi Houvinen is the last rune singer, the *Kalevala* will not die with him. Today, there is a written **7.** _____ of the *Kalevala* for people to read. Also, British author J.R.R. Tolkien (who wrote *The Lord of the Rings*) read the *Kalevala*. Many of the *Kalevala*'s ideas are **8.** _____ in Tolkien's stories. Some characters in Tolkien's books also speak a language similar to the ancient Finnish language used in the *Karevala*.

B. Matching. Match the words from the box in **A** with the correct definition.

1. any written material _____
2. mainly, mostly _____
3. making you feel afraid _____
4. despite _____
5. suitable for a particular person or situation _____
6. a set or group of something _____
7. to show (e.g., in a mirror) _____
8. to learn something so you remember it exactly _____

> **Word Link** We can add **–en** to some adjectives to form verbs. For example, if you *soften* something, you make it soft. Other examples are: *lengthen, strengthen, weaken*.

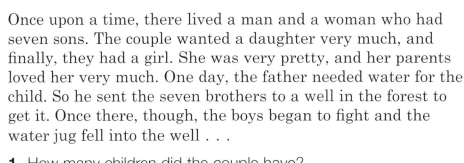

▲ A well in a forest

Before You Read

A. Discussion. Look at the photos and read the paragraph. Then answer the questions below.

Once upon a time, there lived a man and a woman who had seven sons. The couple wanted a daughter very much, and finally, they had a girl. She was very pretty, and her parents loved her very much. One day, the father needed water for the child. So he sent the seven brothers to a well in the forest to get it. Once there, though, the boys began to fight and the water jug fell into the well . . .

1. How many children did the couple have?
2. Why were the brothers in the forest?
3. What happened there?

B. Predict. What do you think happens next in the story? Read the first two paragraphs on the next page to check your ideas. How do you think the story ends? Read the rest of the story to find out.

▲ A jug

The Tale of the Seven Ravens

1   The **youths** looked into the well and thought of their father. They were afraid to go home.

Hours passed. "Where are those boys?" shouted the father angrily. "They are probably playing a game and have
5   forgotten about the water. I wish they were all turned into ravens!" And when he looked up, he saw seven black birds flying away. The father was **shocked**. "What have I done?" he thought. But it was too late. He could not take back his words.

10   In time, the girl grew up and discovered she had brothers. The story of their misfortune[1] **affected** her **deeply**, and she decided to find them. For years she searched and did not stop. She was **determined** to find her brothers. Finally, she found their home. To enter, she needed a special key made from
15   a chicken bone, which she did not have. The girl thought for a moment, and then took a knife and cut off[2] one of her fingers. With it, she opened the front door and went inside. On a table, there were seven plates and seven cups. She ate and drank a little from each. In the last cup, she **accidentally**
20   dropped a ring that her parents had given her.

Eventually, the ravens returned for their meal. The girl **hid** behind the door and watched. When the seventh raven drank from his cup, something hit his mouth. The raven **recognized** it **immediately**—it was his parents' ring. "I wish our sister
25   were here," he said, "and then we could be free." At that moment, their sister ran to them, and **suddenly** the ravens were human again. The brothers kissed their sister, and all eight of them went home together happily.

"...and when he looked up, he saw seven black birds flying away."

[1] **Misfortune** is bad luck.
[2] If you **cut** something **off**, or **cut off** something, you remove it with a knife or a similar tool.

Reading Comprehension

A. Multiple Choice. Choose the best answer for each question.

Gist **1.** What is this story mainly about?
  a. a father who leaves his children
  b. a bad witch who lives in a forest
  c. a sister who saves her brothers
  d. magical birds who help children

Vocabulary **2.** In line 5, what does *turned into* mean?
  a. changed to   c. circled around
  b. interested in   d. returned to

Detail **3.** Why does the girl cut off her finger?
  a. so she can remove a ring from her finger
  b. because her finger is stuck in a door hole
  c. because a bad witch makes her do it
  d. so she can use it to enter the ravens' house

Detail **4.** How do the ravens become human again?
  a. Their sister kisses them.
  b. They eat a magic ring.
  c. One raven makes a wish.
  d. They drink from a special cup.

Inference **5.** What is the moral of this story?
  a. Your parents always know best.
  b. A wish can change your life.
  c. Don't talk to strange people.
  d. Work hard and you will be happy.

B. Sequencing. Put the events below in order from 1– 6. Then retell this story to a partner.

  a. _____ One raven finds the ring and wishes he could see his sister.
  b. _____ The ravens change back into humans and return home with their sister.
  c. _____ The girl finds the house of the seven ravens.
  d. _____ The father makes an angry wish. His sons change into birds.
  e. _____ The girl drops her ring into one of the raven's cups.
  f. _____ The girl learns she has brothers and she searches for them.

Vocabulary Practice

A. Completion. Complete the information with the
correct form of words from the box. One word is extra.

accidentally	determine	deeply
affect	immediately	youth

Sol Guy and Josh Thome want to tell you a story—
a real-life fairy tale. In one story, a poor child grows
up and helps thousands of people in East Africa. In
another, a successful hip-hop artist from Brazil builds
community centers and helps children. These people are
1. _____ to make changes and improve lives.
Guy and Thome's TV show, *4REAL*, tells these
people's stories.

▲ On their TV show, 4REAL,
Josh Thome (left) and Sol
Guy have worked with
actress Cameron Diaz and
rapper Mos Def.

Each *4REAL* show takes a celebrity (an actor or
musician) to a different country. There, the celebrities
meet young people who are helping others. Many of
these **2.** _____ are poor, but they aren't sitting
and waiting for help. They want to do something
3. _____— now, today. Their energy is amazing.

4REAL's stories will **4.** _____ you
5. _____. "Once you see what [these] people are
[doing], you'll never think about these issues in the same way,"
says Thome.

B. Words in Context. Complete each sentence with the best answer.

1. If something happens accidentally, it happens _____.
  a. by chance   b. because you planned it

2. If you hide something, you _____ people to see it.
  a. want   b. don't want

3. If something happens suddenly, it happens _____.
  a. slowly   b. quickly

4. You recognize a person or thing you _____.
  a. know   b. don't know

5. If something shocks you, it surprises you in a _____ way.
  a. bad   b. good

Usage

Effect and **affect** are often
confused. *Effect* is a noun,
affect is a verb. *The earthquake
affected thousands of people.
The scientist studied the effect
of the new medicine on rats.*

Sleepy Hollow

Sleepy Hollow, New York

A. Preview. Look at the stamp. *The Legend of Sleepy Hollow* is a famous American story. Do you know the story? If not, what do you think it might be about?

B. Summarize. Watch the video, *Sleepy Hollow.* Then complete the summary below using words from the box. Three words are extra.

accidentally	affect	although	collection
deeply	recognize	reflect	youth
scary	shocked	suddenly	

Sleepy Hollow is a small town in New York state. It is the setting of a(n) **1.** _____ story called *The Legend of Sleepy Hollow*, written by Washington Irving. Irving visited Sleepy Hollow as a **2.** _____. The young man was **3.** _____ influenced by the town's people and stories. When he grew up, he wrote his famous tale about real people and places from this town.

In the story, a man named Ichabod Crane is riding his horse one night. **4.** _____, another man on a horse begins to follow him. Ichabod doesn't **5.** _____ the man, but as the other rider gets closer, he sees that it is a man with no head—a headless horseman! Ichabod is **6.** _____ and rides away quickly.

7. _____ Irving did not write his story in Sleepy Hollow, he lived in this town as an adult. Today, tourists still visit to see Irving's house (a complete **8.** _____ of his books are here) and to hear *The Legend of Sleepy Hollow* told.

C. Think About It.

1. Would you like to visit Sleepy Hollow? Why or why not?

2. Why do you think so many people like reading or hearing scary stories?

To learn more about stories and storytellers, visit elt.heinle.com/explorer

UNIT 9

Tough Jobs

Discuss these questions with a partner.

1. What do you think the man in the photo is doing?
2. What are some challenging or dangerous jobs? Make a list.
3. Would you like to do any of the jobs you've listed? Why or why not?

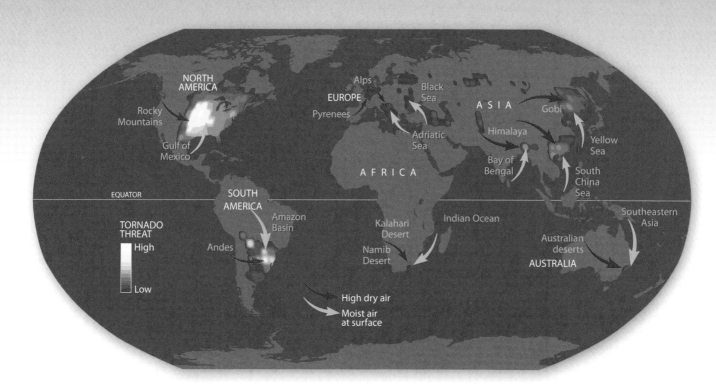

▲ The U.S.A. has about 1,000 tornadoes per year—more than any other country.

9A Wild Weather

Before You Read

A. Matching. Read the information below and match each word in blue with its definition.

- A tornado (or "twister") begins as a storm in the sky and extends down to the ground. A tornado's wind can move at 400 kilometers (250 miles) an hour.
- Most tornado deaths are caused by flying debris (broken buildings, trees, cars, etc.)
- Tornadoes are extremely difficult for meteorologists to predict.

1. broken pieces of something _____
2. people who study the weather _____
3. air moving across the Earth's surface _____
4. bad weather, with wind and rain _____

B. Predict. Look at the title and photo on the next page. What do you think a tornado chaser does? Read the passage to check your ideas.

Tornado Chasers

In the U.S., tornadoes are **responsible** for 80 deaths and more than 1,500 injuries each year. Although they **occur** quite **frequently**, tornadoes are difficult to predict. Why? Tornadoes develop from storms, but only some storms
5   have the **potential** to become tornadoes. Meteorologists don't know where and when a storm will touch the ground and turn into a tornado. Today, the warning time for a tornado is usually just 13 minutes.

Tim Samaras is a storm chaser. His job is to find
10   tornadoes and follow them. When he gets close to a tornado, he puts a special tool called a *turtle probe* on the ground. This tool measures things like a twister's temperature, humidity,[1] and wind speed. With this information, Samaras can learn what causes tornadoes to
15   develop. If meteorologists understand this, they can **warn** people about twisters sooner and save lives.

How does Samaras hunt tornadoes? It's not easy. First, he has to find one. Tornados are too small to see using weather satellites.[2] So Samaras can't **rely on** these tools to find a
20   twister. Instead he waits for tornadoes to develop. Every May and June, Samaras drives about 40,000 kilometers (25,000 miles) across an area known as Tornado Alley, looking and hoping to spot a twister.

Once Samaras sees a tornado, the chase begins. But a
25   tornado is hard to follow. Some tornadoes change **direction** several times—for example, moving east and then west and then east again. When Samaras finally gets near a tornado, he puts the turtle probe on the ground. Being this close to a twister is **terrifying**. Debris is flying in the air. The wind is
30   **blowing** at high speed. He must get away quickly.

The work is risky, even for a **skilled** chaser like Samaras. But danger won't stop his hunt for the perfect storm.

▲ Samaras runs back to his car after placing the turtle probe.

[1] **Humidity** is the amount of water in the air.
[2] A **weather satellite** is a tool that circles the Earth and sends back information about the weather.

Did You Know?

In June 2003, South Dakota experienced 67 tornadoes—in one day!

Reading Comprehension

A. Multiple Choice. Choose the best answer for each question.

Gist **1.** This reading is mainly about a man who _____.
  a. follows tornadoes to learn how they form
  b. predicts when tornadoes will occur around the world
  c. helps people who are hurt by tornadoes
  d. drives tourists around Tornado Alley

Detail **2.** Which statement about tornadoes is true?
  a. Meteorologists use satellites to predict when they will occur.
  b. They usually move in a straight line from place to place.
  c. Meteorologists can't predict exactly where they will form.
  d. People usually have 24 hours to prepare for them.

Detail **3.** A turtle probe _____ tornadoes.
  a. can predict   c. gets information from
  b. chases   d. decreases the power of

Main Idea **4.** What is paragraph 3 mainly about?
  a. how tornadoes develop
  b. how the turtle probe works
  c. how big Tornado Alley is
  d. how Samaras finds a tornado

Vocabulary **5.** In line 23, what does the word *spot* mean?
  a. stop   c. see
  b. place   d. wait for

B. Sequencing. What does a storm chaser like Tim Samaras do? Put the events below in the correct order (1–7).

  ____ puts the turtle probe on the ground
  ____ shares the information with meteorologists
  ____ drives around, looking for tornadoes
  ____ gets close to a tornado
  ____ collects information from the turtle probe to learn how tornadoes form
  ____ sees a tornado and follows it
  ____ moves away quickly

Vocabulary Practice

▲ It's not just Americans who work in cold Arctic weather. These Japanese fishermen, for example, are preparing crabs they have caught in the Bering Sea.

A. Completion. Complete the information with the correct form of words from the box. One word is extra.

blow	direction	frequent	occur	potential
rely on	responsible	skilled	terrifying	warn

Who has probably the most dangerous job in the U.S.A.? A police officer, a miner, a truck driver? No, it's a fisherman—specifically crab fishers in the Bering Sea. Why is this work so difficult? A lot of it is done during winter, when temperatures are extremely cold, and powerful storms **1.** _____ **2.** _____. Strong winds can sometimes **3.** _____ fishermen off their boats into the cold water, and are **4.** _____ for a number of deaths. In the winter, it is also quite dark, even during the day. So fishermen can't **5.** _____ their eyes to help them move in the right **6.** _____ on the boat.

Many people die doing this job every year—the most in the U.S.A. So why do men and women risk their lives to do this **7.** _____ and difficult work? One reason is money. A(n) **8.** _____ fisherman (or woman) has the **9.** _____ to earn U.S. $25,000 for working only five weeks at sea.

B. Definitions. Use the correct form of the words in the box in **A** to complete the definitions.

1. If something happens _____, it happens often.
2. A _____ event is very scary.
3. A _____ worker is experienced and knowledgeable about his or her job.
4. If something _____, it happens.
5. If you can _____ a person or thing, you can trust or depend on them.
6. If bad weather is _____ for many deaths, the weather causes those deaths.
7. When the wind _____, the air moves fast.
8. If you go left and your partner goes right, he moves in the opposite _____.
9. If something has the _____ to happen, it might happen.

Word Link

We can add **–ly** to some adjectives to form adverbs: for example, *frequently, immediately, physically, completely, stylishly.*

Forests on Fire

☐ Before You Read

A. Matching. Look at the map and read the paragraph below. Then match each word in blue with its definition.

Every year around the globe, wildfires burn millions of hectares of land. In Russia, there are more wildfires than anywhere else in the world. Often hot, dry weather and fast-moving winds make these fires more dangerous.

1. to set on fire _____

2. an area of land that is 10,000 square meters _____

3. a fire that is out of control and moves quickly _____

B. Predict. Read the three questions in the headings on the next page. What do you think the answers are? Read the passage to check your ideas.

Arctic Ocean

Moscow ★

R U S S I A
S I B E R I A

▨ Large reported fires, 2001   MONGOLIA   Pacific Ocean

◀ In Russia, there are between 20,000–35,000 wildfires each year.

Smokejumpers

1 Every year, wildfires **destroy** millions of hectares of forest land. Homes are **damaged**, and thousands of people die. Smokejumpers are helping to stop this.

5 ## What is a smokejumper?

Smokejumpers are a special type of firefighter. They jump from planes into areas that are difficult to reach by car or on foot, like the **middle** of a mountain forest. They **race** to
10 put out fires as fast as they can.

What do smokejumpers do?

At a fire site, smokejumpers first examine the land and decide how to fight the fire. Their main goal is to stop a fire from spreading.
15 Using basic **equipment** such as shovels and axes,[1] smokejumpers clear land of burnable[2] material like plants and other dry material. They carry water with them too, but only a limited amount.

20 ## Who can be a smokejumper?

Although the **majority** of smokejumpers are men, more women are joining. Most important are your **height** and weight. Smokejumpers **employed** in the U.S., for example, must be 120 to 200 pounds (54 to 91 kilograms), so they
25 don't get hurt when they land, or get blown by strong winds.

Smokejumpers must also be **capable** of surviving in the wilderness. In Russia, many smokejumpers know how to find food in the forest and even make simple furniture[3] from trees.

The work is dangerous, and the hours are long. But for these
30 firefighters, smokejumping isn't just an **occupation**. They love being able to jump out of planes, fight fires, and live in the forest. As 28-year-old Russian smokejumper Alexi Tishin says, "This is the best job for tough guys."

"We face danger three times: one when we fly; two when we jump; three when we go to [the] fire."

– Valeriy Korotkov, smokejumper

Did You Know?
Russia has the largest number of smokejumpers in the world.

[1] A **shovel** is a tool used for digging earth; an **ax** is a tool used for cutting wood.
[2] If something is **burnable**, it can start a fire easily.
[3] Objects such as chairs, tables, or beds are known as **furniture**.

Reading Comprehension

A. Multiple Choice. Choose the best answer for each question.

Gist **1.** What is the reading mainly about?
   a. the life of a Russian smokejumper
   b. who smokejumpers are and what they do
   c. the difficulties of being a female smokejumper
   d. why people become smokejumpers

Detail **2.** When a smokejumper gets to a fire site, what is the first thing he or she does?
   a. looks for water   c. starts a small fire
   b. clears the land   d. studies the land

Detail **3.** If you want to be a smokejumper, you must be _____.
   a. older than 28   c. within a certain height range
   b. male   d. able to fly a plane

Vocabulary **4.** In a *wilderness* (line 27), there are not many _____.
   a. people   c. trees
   b. fires   d. animals

Inference **5.** In Alexi Tishin's opinion, why do people become smokejumpers?
   a. for the money   c. to help their country
   b. for the excitement   d. to work short hours

Did You Know?
Naturally occurring wildfires are important in nature. They clean forest floors of dead plants and insects and allow new plants to grow.

B. Completion. Complete the job description with information from the reading.

Smokejumper for the Forest Service

Job Description:
Are you a skilled firefighter looking for a new challenge? If so, we have the job for you. As a smokejumper, you will jump into areas that are **1.** _____ to reach. Your main goal will be to stop a fire from **2.** _____.

Both **3.** _____ and _____ can join our team of smokejumpers. But you must . . .

- weigh **4.** _____ kilos
- be able to **5.** _____ in the wilderness independently
- be ready to work **6.** _____ hours

If interested, apply with a resume and cover letter to smokejumperjob@rexplorer.org

Vocabulary Practice

A. Completion. Complete the information with the correct form of words from the box. One word is extra.

capable	employ	equipment	majority
middle	occupation	race	

Eighteen-year-old A.J. Coston is **1.** _____
as a volunteer[1] firefighter. On Saturday nights, he doesn't
sleep much. Several times a night, he has to jump out of
bed and **2.** _____ to help someone. During
the week, he lives with his family. His usual
3. _____ is being a high school student.
But on the weekend, Coston lives and works at the
fire station.

To get the job, Coston had to take classes and learn
different safety skills. He also had to learn to use different
firefighting **4.** _____—axes, special flash
lights, and other tools. When Coston was
5. _____ of using these, he was allowed to
work inside burning buildings.

Although firefighters spend the **6.** _____ of
their time putting out fires, they also sometimes help
people who have had accidents. This, says Coston, is one
of the most important parts of the job.

▲ Part-time firefighter
A.J. Coston

[1] If you **volunteer,** you do work for free.

B. Words in Context. Complete each sentence with the best answer.

1. If you damage something, you _____ it.
a. break
b. fix

2. If you destroy something, it can _____ be used again.
a. now
b. never

3. We measure height in _____.
a. kilograms / pounds
b. centimeters / inches

4. If a book is in the middle of the table, it is _____ of the table.
a. in the center
b. near the edge

> ### Word Link
>
> We can add **–ment**
> to some verbs to form
> nouns. These nouns often
> describe an action,
> process, or state of being
> (*employment,*
> *encouragement*) or an
> object or place (*equipment,*
> *settlement*).

Wildfire Photographer

A. Preview. Look at the photo. What do you think are the good and bad points of Mark Thiessen's job?

▲ Mark Thiessen is a wildfire photographer.

B. Summarize. Watch the video, *Wildfire Photographer*. Then complete the summary below using the correct form of words from the box. Two words are extra.

blow	destroy	direction	frequently	height
occur	majority	middle	occupation	race
responsible	skilled	terrifying		

Every year, huge wildfires **1.** _____ millions of hectares of land in the U.S.A. These fires are **2.** _____ for people being injured or losing their homes.

Mark Thiessen is a *National Geographic* photographer. The **3.** _____ of his pictures are of things like dinosaur bones, or people. But during the summer, he photographs forest fires. He **4.** _____ quickly from place to place, interviewing firefighters and taking pictures.

Now he is in Idaho. Wildfires **5.** _____ here **6.** _____—especially in the hot summer months. Tonight, a powerful wind is **7.** _____, and a huge fire is spreading across the Idaho desert. Suddenly, some parts of the fire come together and start to twist. The result is a "fire tornado." It reaches a(n) **8.** _____ of ten or fifteen meters. It's a(n) **9.** _____ sight.

Mark is a photographer, but he also has a second **10.** _____: he is a(n) **11.** _____ firefighter too—the perfect mix for being a wildfire photographer.

C. Think About It.

1. What are Mark Thiessen's occupations? What skills are important for these jobs?

2. Do you think Mark's work is more or less dangerous than other jobs in this unit?

 To learn more about tough jobs, visit elt.heinle.com/ explorer

A. Crossword. Use the definitions below to complete the missing words.

Across
1. quickly; unexpectedly
6. to study something carefully
7. the weather in a certain place
9. entirely
11. a young person
12. right away; now
13. correct or suitable for a situation
16. to look for or search for something
17. to happen
18. to guess the value

Down
1. very fast
2. experienced
3. a very large or tall person or thing
4. often
5. any written material
7. a group of similar things
8. tools used for a certain job
10. to learn something so you remember it exactly
14. a competition to see who is the fastest
15. to tell someone about a possible danger

B. Notes Completion. Scan the information on pages 108–109 to complete the notes.

Field Notes

Site: Fiordland

Location: South Island of _____

Information:
- National Park has many rare kinds of flowers, plants, and _____
- Important site of legends for local _____ people
- New Zealand had no native _____ —introduced later by foreigners
- First Europeans, led by James _____, came in year _____
- Many native birds, e.g. the _____ (symbol of New Zealand), are endangered
- Now fewer than _____ kakapo birds left in the wild
- Visitors can walk more than _____ km of walking paths
- Other tourists see fiords by _____ or _____

Land of Legends

Site: **Fiordland**

Location: **South Island, New Zealand**

Category: **Natural**

Status: **World Heritage Site since 1990**

"The Eighth Wonder of the World"

British writer Rudyard Kipling's opinion of Fiordland after visiting the area in 1891

Fiordland National Park on New Zealand's South Island is like an outdoor museum: the area is home to hundreds of native plants, flowers, and animals that cannot be found anywhere else in the world. The most amazing thing in Fiordland, though, is the magical sight of the fiords themselves—narrow strips of water, some over 200 meters deep, that cut between the high mountains facing the coast.

For centuries, New Zealand's native Maori were the only people who knew about Fiordland. They took trips there to hunt animals and to collect greenstone. Fiordland has since become an important part of local Maori legends. The first Europeans arrived in 1778, when ships led by James Cook came to explore the coast of New Zealand. The majority of today's travelers come to enjoy over 480 kilometers (300 miles) of walking paths. Tourists who enjoy riskier activities can explore the fiords by kayak or helicopter. However they are viewed, the reflections on the surface of New Zealand's famous fiords are always a magical sight.

Glossary

endangered: in danger of dying out completely
greenstone: a dark green rock used for making jewelry and statues

▲ A native Maori wears a cloak made of kiwi feathers.

Local Legends

Maori legend says that a god named Tu-te-raki-whanoa cut the coastline, making the fiords so that people could settle the land. Today visitors may recognize Fiordland from a more recent example of storytelling: from 2001–2003, the park was used for scenes of "Middle Earth" in the popular film series *Lord of the Rings*, directed by New Zealander Peter Jackson.

Birds in Danger

Until the first European visitors introduced foreign animals to New Zealand there were no natural predators. Because they were not hunted, many of New Zealand's native birds are now physically unable to fly. These include the kiwi, the takahe, and the kakapo (a giant parrot that smells of flowers!). These birds must now rely on their speedy legs to quickly find places to hide from predators. Many are rare; some are now in danger of dying out completely.

The **kiwi**—the national symbol of New Zealand—is a relative of the extinct moa, a giant 3.6-meter (12 foot) bird that died out more than 500 years ago.

The **kakapo** is the most endangered parrot in the world—there are fewer than 100 left in the wild.

In 1948, people in Fiordland suddenly discovered hundreds of **takahe**, a bird that had not been seen for more than 50 years.

A. Word Link. The suffix **–ment** changes verbs (e.g., *employ*) into nouns (e.g., *employment*). Read sentences **1–5** below. Then, complete sentences **a–e** with the noun form of the verbs in **red**.

1. One way to **improve** your English is to live in an English-speaking country.
2. Different companies **advertise** their products in newspapers and magazines.
3. Russian smokejumpers are **paid** about 3,100 rubles (100 U.S. dollars) per month.
4. When scientists **measured** the dinosaur's arms, they were 2.4 meters (eight feet) long.
5. The city plans to **invest** money in a new tornado warning system.

a. There is an _____ for travel to Panama in this month's magazine.
b. Europe uses the metric system of _____ to describe distance and weight.
c. By the end of the course, many students see an _____ in their reading skills.
d. Buying property is often a good _____.
e. Renting the room costs 900 euros per month. Each _____ is due on the first day of the month.

B. Word Partnership. Read the passage below and underline ***be* + adjective + preposition** combinations, for example: "was determined to". Then match the parts of the sentences below.

▲ National Geographic Emerging Explorer Alexandra Cousteau
© 2008 National Geographic

Alexandra Cousteau is related to the French oceanographer Jacques Cousteau. Jacques explored the world's oceans and invented a number of underwater tools, including scuba-diving equipment. Like her grandfather, Alexandra is concerned about the future of the world's oceans and our water resources. Many people are familiar with these problems, she says. But just telling people the facts doesn't lead to action. Alexandra is interested in telling real stories about how people are using or protecting water supplies. By making the issues personal, she says, people are more likely to care. "That's why my grandfather was so successful," she says. "He wasn't [just] an oceanographer; he was [also] a [great] storyteller." Alexandra also wants to create video games about water and climate for youths. Like her famous grandfather, she's committed to teaching both young and old people about our planet's most important resource: water.

1. Alexandra Cousteau is related to	**a.** stories about water protection
2. She is concerned about	**b.** the education of people of different ages
3. She says many people are familiar with	**c.** Jacques Cousteau
4. She is interested in	**d.** the oceans and other water resources
5. She is committed to	**e.** the problems she talks about

UNIT 10

Pyramid Builders

Discuss these questions with a partner.

1. What is a pyramid? Where can you see pyramids?
2. Why do you think people built pyramids?
3. What is one of the oldest buildings in your city or country? How old is it? Why was it built?

▲ The Temple of the Great Jaguar in Tikal, Guatemala, once held the tomb of a Mayan king.

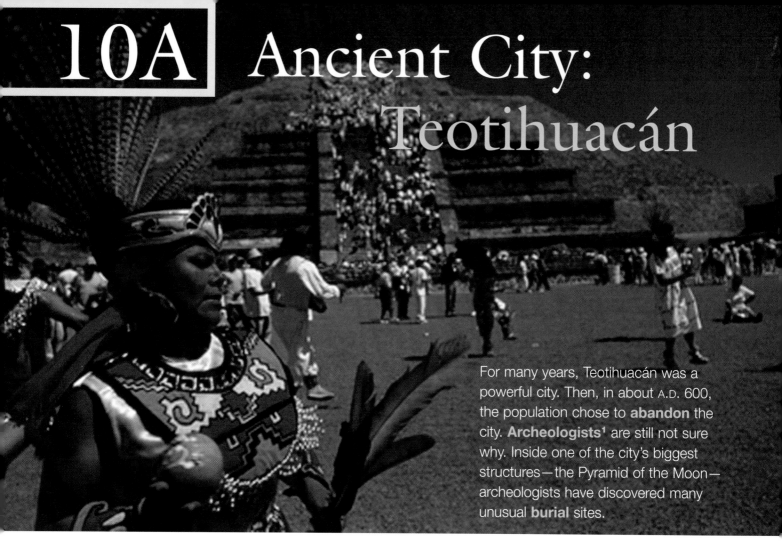

10A Ancient City: Teotihuacán

For many years, Teotihuacán was a powerful city. Then, in about A.D. 600, the population chose to **abandon** the city. **Archeologists**[1] are still not sure why. Inside one of the city's biggest structures—the Pyramid of the Moon— archeologists have discovered many unusual **burial** sites.

▲ Performers recreate an ancient religious ceremony at Teotihuacán's Pyramid of the Moon.

Before You Read

A. Matching. Read the information above and match each word in blue with its definition.

1. placing of a dead person's body into the ground or a tomb

   _____

2. scientists who study buildings, tools, and other objects from the past _____

3. leave a place, thing, or person suddenly, usually forever

   _____

B. Predict. Look at the photo and caption on the next page. What did archeologists find in the Pyramid of the Moon? What might they learn from these things? Read the passage to check your ideas.

[1] **Archeologist** can also be spelled **archaeologist**.

MEXICO'S
PYRAMID OF THE MOON

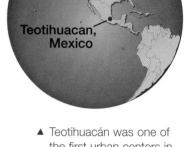

Teotihuacan, Mexico

▲ Teotihuacán was one of the first urban centers in the Americas.

A Mysterious City

Teotihuacán (tay-o-tee-hwah-KAHN) was once one of the world's most important cities, but many things about it are still unknown today. How did the people
5 live, and why did they abandon their city? For years, answers to some of these questions have been buried in the Pyramid of the Moon. Now, findings in this ancient **structure** are helping archeologists learn more about Teotihuacán's people and their culture.

Clues in the Pyramid
10 Until recently, many **experts** thought Teotihuacán was a peaceful society, mostly ruled by gentle and **wise** leaders. But recent findings in the Pyramid of the Moon **indicate** something else. Archeologists discovered a number of
15 headless bodies. Most were foreigners. Many had their hands tied and were buried alive, along with animals, weapons,[1] and other objects of power. **Apparently** the people and objects found inside the pyramid were **offerings** to the gods.

▲ An archeologist working inside the pyramid unearths human bones—evidence of ancient sacrifice.

20 However, the findings in the pyramid are difficult to **interpret**. "[These findings] are like sentences," says archeologist Leonardo Lopez Lujan, "but we don't have all the words . . . so they're hard to read." Despite these problems, several archeologists have **concluded** this: Teotihuacán was not a society **governed** by
25 peaceful rulers. In reality, **officials** used human sacrifice,[2] says archeologist Saburo Sugiyama, "to control the people." The city probably also had a powerful army.[3]

The Search Goes On
Who were the city's leaders? Scientists don't know. They
30 have not found a king buried in the pyramid or any statues of Teotihuacán's rulers. But archeologists continue to search for them. They hope to learn more about the pyramid's creators and one of the world's most powerful ancient cities.

" . . . [These findings] are like sentences but we don't have all the words . . . so they're hard to read."

[1] A **weapon** is an object used to kill others, like a gun or a knife.
[2] **Human sacrifice** is the killing of a person as an offering to a god.
[3] An **army** is a group of people who fight in a war.

Reading Comprehension

A. Multiple Choice. Choose the best answer for each question.

Gist **1.** What is the reading mainly about?
   a. how the Pyramid of the Moon was built
   b. discoveries in the Pyramid of the Moon
   c. a king who built the Pyramid of the Moon
   d. why the people of Teotihuacán left their city

Vocabulary **2.** In line 10, what does the word *clues* mean?
   a. questions   b. findings   c. archeologists   d. gods

Detail **3.** What have NOT been found in the Pyramid of the Moon?
   a. the bodies of kings   c. weapons
   b. human skeletons   d. animal skeletons

Inference **4.** In line 21, an archeologist says, "*[These findings] are like sentences but we don't have all the words . . . so they're hard to read.*" What does he mean?
   a. There is writing in the pyramid, but no one can read it.
   b. We don't fully understand the findings in the pyramid yet.
   c. We have not made any discoveries in Teotihuacán yet.
   d. The Teotihuacán language did not have many words.

Reference **5.** In line 32, what does *them* refer to?
   a. archeologists   b. pyramids   c. cities   d. kings

B. True or False. Read the sentences below and circle **T** (True) or **F** (False).

1. The people and animals in the pyramid died in a religious ceremony.   **T   F**

2. Rulers sacrificed humans to control the people of Teotihuacán.   **T   F**

3. Teotihuacán had a small army.   **T   F**

4. Most of the dead bodies found in the pyramid were people from Teotihuacán.   **T   F**

Tourists climb down a pyramid ▶
in Teotihuacán, Mexico.

Vocabulary Practice

A. Completion. Complete the information with the correct form of words from the box. One word is extra.

▲ The man who started a Mayan dynasty: Fire Is Born

apparently	govern	interpret	wise
expert	indicate	structure	

The rainforests of Central America were once home to millions of people called the Maya. These people had advanced systems of mathematics, writing, and astronomy. They also built great cities and huge **1.** _____, like the pyramids of Chichén Itzá, now in Mexico. The Maya shared a common culture, but they did not have a single city capital or ruler. Instead, each Mayan city **2.** _____ itself.

How did this collection of cities become one of the greatest cultures in the Americas? Many **3.** _____ now believe a man from Teotihuacán named "Fire Is Born" was responsible. Recent findings **4.** _____ that he arrived in the Mayan city of Waka in Guatemala on January 8, A.D. 378 with his army. He then took control of Tikal—one of the most important Mayan cities. What kind of leader was he? **5.** _____, Fire is Born encouraged trade and communication with other cities and cultures throughout the region. Today, many believe this **6.** _____ leader from Teotihuacán strongly influenced the Mayan world.

B. Words in Context. Complete each sentence with the best answer.

1. If you conclude that something is true, you decide this _____ you study the facts.
   a. before   b. after

2. If a sentence in English is difficult to interpret, it is hard to _____.
   a. understand   b. write

3. An offering is something you _____ someone.
   a. take from   b. give to

4. An official is a(n) _____ person in an organization or government.
   a. important   b. unimportant

Word Link

We can add **–ate** to words to form verbs, e.g., *indicate* (to show or identify), *activate* (to make something start working).

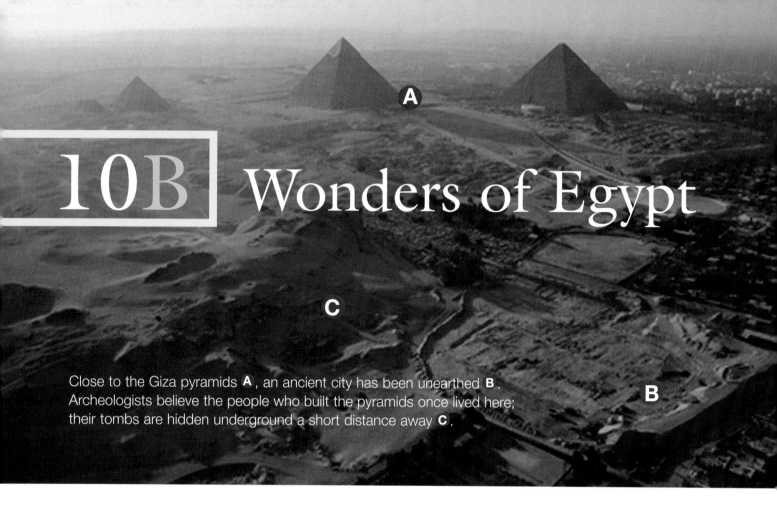

Wonders of Egypt

Close to the Giza pyramids **A**, an ancient city has been unearthed **B**.
Archeologists believe the people who built the pyramids once lived here;
their tombs are hidden underground a short distance away **C**.

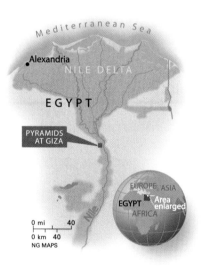

Before You Read

A. True or False. Read the sentences below and circle
T (True) or **F** (False). Then check your answers on page 120.

1. The pyramids at Giza are older than the pyramids of
   Central America.   **T F**
2. When they were first built, the pyramids at Giza were white.   **T F**
3. The Great Pyramid of Khufu at Giza was the world's tallest
   structure for over 3,000 years.   **T F**

B. Predict. Read the photo caption above and skim the reading
on the next page. Who do you think built the Giza pyramids?
Circle your answer. Then read the passage to check.

a. foreign workers
b. foreign slaves
c. Egyptian workers
d. Egyptian slaves

Who Built Giza's Pyramids?

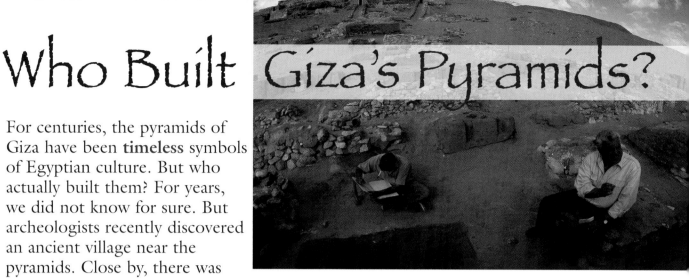

1   For centuries, the pyramids of Giza have been **timeless** symbols of Egyptian culture. But who actually built them? For years,
5   we did not know for sure. But archeologists recently discovered an ancient village near the pyramids. Close by, there was also a cemetery where pyramid builders were buried. From
10   studying these places, archeologists can now **confirm** that the pyramids were not built by slaves or foreigners (or space aliens!). **Ordinary** Egyptians built them.

▲ Archeologist Dr. Zahi Hawass led the team that discovered the pyramid builders' tombs.

  It took about eighty years to build the pyramids. **According** to archeologists, about 20,000–30,000 people
15   were **involved** in completing the **task**. The workers had different **roles**. Some dug up[1] the rock, some moved it, and some shaped it into **blocks**. People also worked on different teams, each with its own name. On a wall in Khufu's Great Pyramid, for example, a group of workers
20   wrote "Friends of Khufu." Teams often **competed** to do a job faster.

  Life for these workers was hard. "We can see that in their skeletons," says Azza Mohamed Sarry El-Din, a scientist studying bodies found in the cemetery. The bones show signs
25   of arthritis,[2] which developed from carrying heavy things for a long time. Archeologists have also found many female skeletons in the village and cemetery. The damage to their bones is similar to the men's. Their lives may have been even tougher: male workers lived to age 40–45, but women to only
30   30–35. However, workers usually had enough food, and they also had medical care if they got sick or hurt.

▲ To build the pyramids, teams of workers carried huge stone blocks up a long ramp.

  The work was challenging, but laborers were **proud** of their work. "It's because they were not just building the tomb of their king," says Egyptian archeologist Zahi Hawass. "They
35   were building Egypt. It was a national project, and everyone was a participant."[3]

[1] If you **dig up** something (or **dig** something **up**), you take it out of the ground.
[2] **Arthritis** is an illness that causes the hands, knees, or other joints to hurt.
[3] A **participant** is a person who joins a certain activity.

Reading Comprehension

A. Multiple Choice. Choose the best answer for each question.

Purpose **1.** The main purpose of this reading is to describe _____.
   a. who the pyramid builders were and what they did
   b. how Khufu's Great Pyramid was constructed
   c. what life was like for Egyptian kings
   d. why Egyptian kings wanted to build pyramids

Detail **2.** Which statement about the pyramid builders is true?
   a. They lived fairly long lives.
   b. Both men and women built the pyramids.
   c. Most came from other countries.
   d. They rarely had enough to eat or drink.

Detail **3.** Which statement about building the pyramids is true?
   a. It took over a century to complete.
   b. Builders all did the same work.
   c. More than 30,000 workers were involved.
   d. Builders worked in teams.

Reference **4.** In line 27, what does *their* refer to?
   a. archeologists   c. female workers
   b. male workers   d. medical workers

Vocabulary **5.** In line 32, what does the word *laborers* mean?
   a. kings   b. archeologists   c. workers   d. women

B. Matching. What is the main idea of each paragraph in the reading? Match a heading (a–e) with the correct paragraph (1–4). One heading is extra.

Paragraph	Heading
1. _____	**a.** A Pyramid Builder's Life
2. _____	**b.** An Important National Project
3. _____	**c.** Female Pyramid Builders: The Challenges
4. _____	**d.** Pyramid Builders' Jobs
	e. Who Built the Pyramids?

Vocabulary Practice

A. Completion. Complete the information with the correct form of words from the box. Three words are extra.

according	compete	involve	proud	task
block	confirm	ordinary	role	timeless

Cleopatra was no **1.** _____ leader. Although she ruled Egypt over 2,000 years ago, her name and her story are still well known today.

Cleopatra became queen at age 18, when her brother became king. The couple **2.** _____ for control of Egypt, and Cleopatra lost. Later, two important leaders from Rome—Julius Caesar and Marc Antony—both fell in love with her. **3.** _____ to legend, Cleopatra was very beautiful. She was also apparently very smart. She used Caesar and Antony to help establish her **4.** _____ as Egyptian queen.

▲ A couple dressed as Caesar and Cleopatra greet visitors at a Las Vegas hotel (U.S.A.).

But staying in power was not an easy **5.** _____. Cleopatra had many enemies[1] who eventually took power from her. In the end, the queen was too **6.** _____ to surrender[2] to her enemies, and instead chose to kill herself. Her legend survived, however, and today Cleopatra remains a(n) **7.** _____ symbol of ancient Egypt.

[1] An **enemy** is someone who hates you or wants to harm you.
[2] If you **surrender**, you say you have lost.

B. Definitions. Use the correct form of the words in the box in **A** to complete the definitions.

1. If something or someone is _____, it is common or usual.
2. A(n) _____ is an activity or some kind of work you do.
3. If something or someone is _____, they are the same forever; they don't change.
4. Your _____ is your job or position.
5. If something is _____, it is shown to be true.
6. A(n) _____ person has strong feelings of self-worth or self-importance.
7. If two people _____ for something, they try to win and get it for themselves.
8. "_____ to" means "as said by someone or something."

> ## Word Partnership
>
> Use *task* with:
> (v.) **complete** a task, **give someone** a task, **face** a task, **perform** a task
> (adj.) **difficult** task, **easy** task, **important** task, **impossible** task, **simple** task.

Giza Pyramids

A. Preview. Look at the photos and read the captions. What kinds of problems do you think are affecting the Giza pyramids today?

▲ Crowds of tourists come to see the pyramids and buy souvenirs of their visit.

◄ Every year the city of Cairo moves closer to Giza's famous monuments.

B. Summarize. Watch the video, *Giza Pyramids.* Then complete the summary below using the correct form of words from the box. Two words are extra.

according to	expert	proud	task
compete	official	role	timeless
conclude	ordinary	structure	wise

Near the pyramids at Giza, a huge wall is being built. What is the purpose of this **1.** _____? Zahi Hawass is a(n) **2.** _____ in Egyptian archeology. **3.** _____ him, a terrible thing is happening in Giza. Near the pyramids, camels and horses are everywhere. Merchants **4.** _____ to sell souvenirs to tourists. Many people act like these monuments—the pyramids and the Sphinx—are **5.** _____ structures. But they are very special. They are **6.** _____—they have existed for over 4,000 years. And Egyptians are **7.** _____ of this history. The wall, says Hawass, will keep out souvenir sellers and animals. Then visitors will be able to feel this place's magic.

Also today in Giza, houses are built almost right next to the pyramids! The city **8.** _____ cannot pull down the buildings, but they can put up a wall to protect the pyramids. Building the wall is a(n) **9.** _____ thing to do, says Hawass. If the important **10.** _____ of building the wall is not complete soon, the magic of the pyramids may be gone in a hundred years.

C. Think About It.

1. Do you think building the wall is a good idea? Why or why not?

2. Which old buildings or structures in your country most need to be protected? Why and how do you think they should be protected?

Answers to Before You Read, page 116:

1. True. They were built over 4,000 years ago—starting in about 2550 B.C.; **2.** True. The top of one of the pyramids still has its white-colored covering.; **3.** True. It was the tallest structure for 3,800 years—until England's Lincoln Cathedral was built in about A.D. 1300.

To learn more about pyramid builders, visit elt.heinle.com/explorer

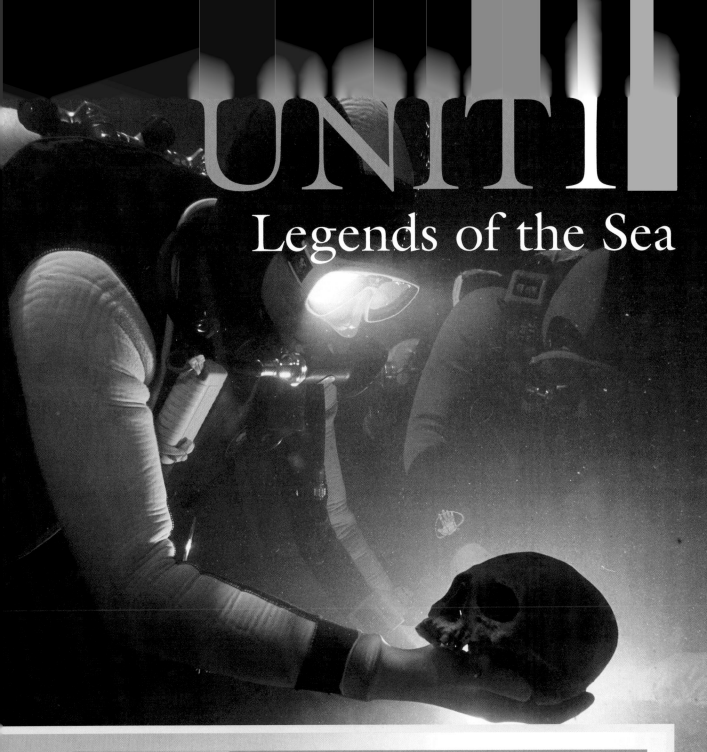

UNIT 11
Legends of the Sea

▲ A diver discovers a human skull underwater
in the Northern Yucatan Peninsula, Mexico.

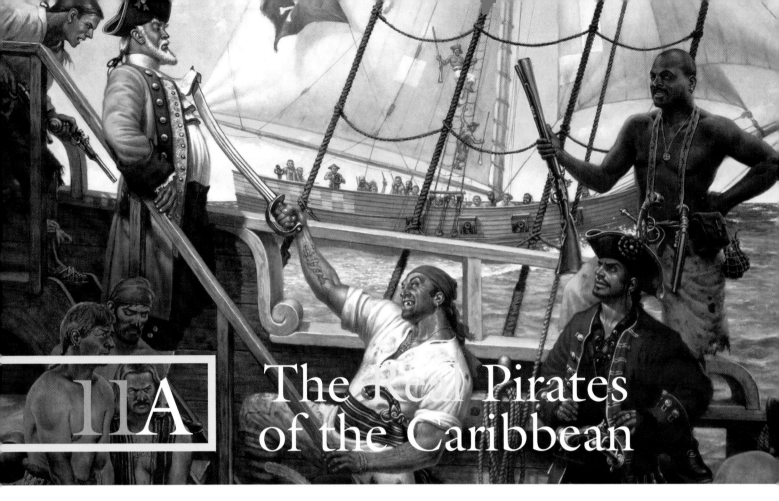

11A The Real Pirates of the Caribbean

▲ Captain Samuel Bellamy (in the red coat) and his pirates take another ship.

Before You Read

A. Matching. Read the information below and match each word in **blue** with its definition.

The Golden Age of Piracy (1660–1730)

- During the period 1660–1730, there was a lot of **maritime** trade between Europe, Africa, the Caribbean, and the eastern coasts of the Americas. Some **goods** commonly traded were cloth, spices, and weapons.

- By the 1720s, pirates were common—especially in the Caribbean.

- Each pirate ship was led by a **captain**. One of the most famous was Black Sam Bellamy (pictured).

   1. the leader of the people on a ship _____

   2. related to the sea _____

   3. things that are made to be sold _____

B. Predict. What do you think pirates were really like? Read the sentences and circle **T** (True) or **F** (False). Then read the passage to check your ideas.

   1. Only the captain made the ship's rules.   **T**   **F**
   2. Pirates made most of their money by stealing gold.   **T**   **F**
   3. Many pirates had wooden legs or wore earrings.   **T**   **F**

PIRATES:
ROMANCE
AND REALITY

▲ A chest of treasure from Black Sam Bellamy's pirate ship, the *Whydah*

1 In many movies, a pirate's life is an exciting adventure. But what was life actually like for an 18th-century pirate? And which parts of the movie pirate are real and which are invented?

A PIRATE'S LIFE

5 In reality, the **average** pirate was usually trying to escape from a difficult life. Some were ex-sailors who were treated poorly on their ships. Others were escaped slaves who wanted their **freedom**. They came from
10 many different backgrounds. But on a pirate ship, **equality** was important. Men elected[1] their captain and created the ship's rules together. The men also **divided** the **income** from stolen goods, and they shared these earnings fairly.

PIRATE TREASURE

15 In popular culture, pirates are often shown with chests full of gold. It is true they took money from others. However, it was far more common for pirates to **steal** things like cloth, spices, and even medicine. Then they often sold these things. Of course, **purchasing** stolen goods from pirates was
20 **illegal**, but many people did it. Also, unlike movie pirates, real "pirates didn't bury their money," says Cori Convertito, who works at a maritime museum in the U.S. "They blew it as soon as they could on women and booze."[2]

PIRATE STYLE

25 Movie pirates often wear eye patches and have wooden legs. In reality, many pirates did look like this. Why? One **factor** was the poor living conditions. "Life at sea was hard and dangerous," says David Moore, a maritime museum employee in the U.S. **Disease** was also common. For these reasons,
30 some pirates lost eyes and legs. But many pirates did one thing for their health: they wore earrings—just as in the movies. They believed putting weight on the ears stopped seasickness.

▲ Around 1700, a French pirate was the first to use a black flag with a skull and crossbones, later known as the Jolly Roger.

[1] If you **elect** someone, you choose that person to lead.
[2] **Booze** is an informal word meaning *alcohol*.

Reading Comprehension

A. Multiple Choice. Choose the best answer for each question.

Main Idea **1.** What is the main idea of this reading?
  a. A pirate's life was a dangerous but exciting adventure.
  b. Some things we've seen or read about pirates are true, but others aren't.
  c. The lives of 18th-century pirates and modern-day pirates are similar.
  d. Today's stories and movies about pirates are entirely wrong.

Detail **2.** On many pirate ships, _____.
  a. men were like slaves
  b. there were several captains
  c. only ex-sailors were allowed
  d. the men shared the money they made

Vocabulary **3.** In line 22, "They blew it" means "They _____ the money."
  a. hid   c. made
  b. spent   d. saved

Inference **4.** Which statement would David Moore probably agree with?
  a. Many pirates had a difficult life and probably died young.
  b. The appearance of movie pirates is very different from reality.
  c. A pirate's life wasn't as dangerous as we see in the movies.
  d. Many pirates were friendlier than we see in the movies.

Detail **5.** According to the passage, pirates believed wearing earrings _____.
  a. was fashionable   c. brought good luck
  b. stopped illness   d. was only for women

B. Classification. Match each answer (a–g) with the type of pirate it describes.

Movie Pirates   **Real Pirates**

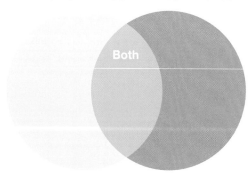

Both

  a. became pirates to have an adventure
  b. wore earrings
  c. stole money
  d. joined pirate ships to escape a difficult life
  e. buried their treasure
  f. stole things like food and medicine
  g. sold their goods and spent their earnings

Vocabulary Practice

A. Completion. Complete the information with the correct form of words from the box. Three words are extra.

average	divide	disease	equality
factor	freedom	illegal	income
purchase	steal		

Most people earn a(n) **1.** _____ by going to work. Not Barry Clifford. He makes money by finding lost pirate treasure. In 1984, he discovered a pirate ship called the *Whydah* in waters near Massachusetts in the U.S.A.

The *Whydah* was an English slave ship. It traveled to western Africa, and the ship's captain **2.** _____ a number of slaves who had lost their **3.** _____. The ship then traveled to the Caribbean. Here, in February 1717, Captain Sam Bellamy and his pirates took the *Whydah*. They **4.** _____ the ship and all of its goods. Later Bellamy's men **5.** _____ the goods among themselves. But their luck didn't last. On April 26, the *Whydah* sank[1] in a storm near Massachusetts, and all but two pirates died.

Today, **6.** _____ such as bad weather and rough water make it difficult for Clifford's team to bring objects up from the *Whydah*. Despite this, over 100,000 objects have been found, including coins, weapons, and clothing. From the pirates' clothes, scientists have learned that the **7.** _____ pirate was only about 1.6 meters tall (5'4"). In other words, most pirates were not as tall as we see in the movies.

[1] If something **sinks**, it goes underwater.

▲ A diver studies a coin discovered from the *Whydah*.

B. Definitions. Use words from the box in **A** to complete the definitions.

1. If you _____ something, you buy it.
2. If you _____ something, you break it into smaller, equal parts.
3. A _____ is a reason or cause of something.
4. If something is _____, it is not allowed by law.
5. _____ is the ability to do, say, or think what you want.
6. _____ is money you earn, usually for work you do.

Word Link We can add **il-** and **ir-** to some words to show an opposite meaning. For example, *illegal* means *not legal*. Other examples include *irregular* and *irresponsible*.

11B Famous Pirates

◄ A man dressed as pirate Edward Teach welcomes visitors to a festival in Maine, U.S.A.

Before You Read

A. Completion. Read the paragraph and then complete the sentences below.

The Golden Age of Piracy produced a number of famous pirates. Edward Teach, better known as Blackbeard, was one of the most famous—and terrifying—pirates of the time. According to legend, he cut off people's fingers and killed others just for fun. From 1716 to 1718, he attacked boats in the Atlantic and the Caribbean. By 1718, he had a large fleet of ships and was the captain of hundreds of pirates. In 1718, the British finally captured and killed Blackbeard.

1. If you *attack* a person or thing, you try to _____ them.
  a. hurt   b. help

2. A *fleet* is an organized group of _____.
  a. ships   b. people

3. If you *capture* something or someone, you _____ them.
  a. take and control   b. free

B. Predict. On the next page, look at the title and headings, and read the first sentence of each paragraph. Answer the questions below. Then read the passage to check your answers.

1. Why do you think the women became pirates?
2. What do you think happened to them?

Women of the Waves

Throughout history, the majority of pirates have been men. But were there any women pirates? Absolutely! Below are two from different parts of the world.

MARY READ: PIRATE IN DISGUISE

Mary Read was born in England around 1690. She lived most of her life disguised as a man. As a teenager, looking for adventure, she dressed as a boy and got a job at sea. Later, as a young woman (still **pretending** to be a man), she got work on a ship and **sailed** to the Caribbean.

On one journey, pirates attacked Mary's ship. Instead of fighting, she joined them. But Mary had to be careful because many pirate ships had a rule: no women allowed. If the men discovered her true identity, they might **shoot** and kill her. So at first Mary stayed by herself and **avoided** the others. But one day, she made a surprising discovery: one of the pirates on the ship was actually a woman! Anne Bonny was the captain's girlfriend, but she was also a pirate herself. Mary told Anne her secret, and the two women became good friends, and powerful fighters. They fought together until they were captured in 1720.

CHING SHIH: PIRATE QUEEN

In the early 1800s, pirate Ching Shih terrorized the Chinese coast. When her powerful pirate husband died, control of his 500 junks **transferred** to Ching Shih. While she was **boss**, her fleet grew to almost 2,000 ships.

A **fearless** fighter, Ching Shih led nearly 80,000 pirates— both men and women. They **targeted** ships and towns along the coast of China. For years, leaders throughout the region **failed** to stop her. Eventually, Ching Shih retired,[1] a rich and **respected** woman.

---

[1] If you **retire**, you stop working completely.

▲ Ching Shih controlled almost 2,000 junks.

Reading Comprehension

A. Multiple Choice. Choose the best answer for each question.

Purpose **1.** What is the main purpose of this reading?
a. to describe two female pirates
b. to compare male and female pirates
c. to describe the challenges that pirates faced
d. to show that female pirates were very common

Vocabulary **2.** Look at the word *disguised* in line 6. Here, *disguise* means to _____.
a. wear beautiful clothes
b. change your appearance
c. hide your feelings
d. look for adventure

Reference **3.** In line 14, what does *others* refer to?
a. ships   b. pirates   c. women   d. rules

Detail **4.** What unusual discovery did Mary Read make?
a. The captain was a woman.
b. Women weren't allowed on pirate ships.
c. The captain was her father.
d. Another pirate was actually a woman.

Detail **5.** Which statement about Ching Shih's ships is NOT true?
a. All of the sailors were women.
b. There were about 2,000 of them.
c. Both male and female pirates worked on them.
d. There were almost 80,000 people on them.

B. Classification. Match each answer (a–g) with the person it describes.

Mary Read   **Ching Shih**

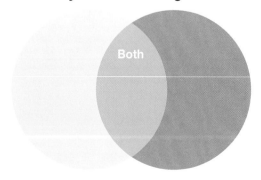

Both

a. was married to a pirate
b. was a pirate during the early 1800s
c. dressed as a man
d. was a skilled fighter
e. became a pirate when her ship was attacked
f. was captured
g. was captain of many ships

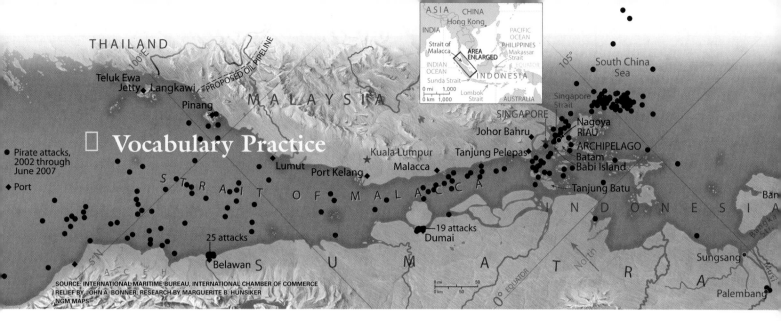

THAILAND

Teluk Ewa
Jetty Langkawi PROPOSED OIL PIPELINE

Pinang

MALAYSIA

□ **Vocabulary Practice**

- Pirate attacks, 2002 through June 2007
- Port

Lumut
Port Kelang
Kuala Lumpur
Malacca
Tanjung Pelepas

Johor Bahru

SINGAPORE

Nagoya
RIAU
ARCHIPELAGO
Batam
Babi Island

Tanjung Batu

STRAIT OF MALACCA

25 attacks
Belawan

ACEH

19 attacks
Dumai

SUMATRA

INDONESIA

Sungsang

Palembang

SOURCE: INTERNATIONAL MARITIME BUREAU, INTERNATIONAL CHAMBER OF COMMERCE
RELIEF BY JOHN A. BONNER; RESEARCH BY MARGUERITE B. HUNSIKER
NGM MAPS

ASIA CHINA
Hong Kong
INDIA
Strait of Malacca AREA ENLARGED
INDIAN OCEAN
Sunda Strait
PACIFIC OCEAN
PHILIPPINES
Makassar Strait
INDONESIA
EQUATOR
Lombok Strait
AUSTRALIA
Singapore Strait
South China Sea

A. Completion. Complete the information with the correct form of words from the box. One word is extra.

▲ Pirate attacks are still common today in the Strait of Malacca.

Pirates might seem like a thing of the past. In reality, they are still common today in places such as the Strait of Malacca in Southeast Asia. This is one of the world's most important shipping regions. Every year, about 70,000 cargo ships **1.** _____ through this area. Today's pirates have better weapons, faster boats, and are **2.** _____ killers. They mostly **3.** _____ cargo ships—for both the goods and the money on board. Some things today's pirates steal (and resell) are oil, wood, animals, and weapons.

| avoid |
| fearless |
| pretend |
| sail |
| shoot |
| target |
| transfer |

How do modern-day pirates work? Sometimes, pirates **4.** _____ to be a ship in trouble. When another ship comes to help, the pirates attack and steal money and goods. Sometimes, pirates use several boats to attack a ship. Two boats go to the back of a ship, one goes in front. When the ship slows to **5.** _____ hitting the boat in front, pirates in the back can easily get on the ship. Pirates will also capture people (for example, tourists or sailors) and hold them. The pirates say they will **6.** _____ the people if they don't get money.

B. Words in Context. Read the sentences and circle **T** (True) or **F** (False).

1. At work, the boss is the lowest person in the office. **T F**

2. If police fail to catch a killer, the police are successful and catch the killer. **T F**

3. If you respect someone, you like and think highly of the person. **T F**

4. If you transfer from one bus to another, you change buses. **T F**

Word Link We can add **trans-** to certain words to show that something moves or changes from one state or place to another (*They transferred the goods from one ship to another ship.*) Other examples include: *transport, transatlantic.*

Blackbeard's Cannons

A. Preview. Look at the photo and answer the questions.

- What is the thing in the picture?
- Why do you think archeologists are interested in it?

B. Summarize. Watch the video, *Blackbeard's Cannons*. Then complete the summary below using the correct form of words from the box. Three words are extra.

▲ Objects brought up from Blackbeard's ship include this 18th-century ship's cannon.

average	boss	divide	factor
fearless	sail	shoot	steal
target	transfer		

Near North Carolina, archeologists have found the wreck[1] of a ship. But this isn't an **1.** _____ ship. Archeologists think it belonged to the most terrifying and **2.** _____ pirate ever: Blackbeard.

In 1717, Blackbeard was **3.** _____ along the coast of North Carolina. He captured a French ship and renamed it *Queen Anne's Revenge*. In 1718, the ship sank. Now, archaeologists think they have found one of the ship's cannons—the large guns used to **4.** _____ at other ships.

When the cannon is pulled up, it doesn't look like a cannon at all. It has been in the water for a long time and is covered in rocks, dirt, and shells. But to project **5.** _____ Mike Ramsing, who leads the team, the cannon is beautiful.

Was this cannon really from Blackbeard's ship? To answer this question, archeologists hope to find the word *Concorde* on the cannon. *Concorde* was the original name of the French ship Blackbeard **6.** _____. Now that the cannon is out of the water, it has been **7.** _____ to a place where it will be cleaned and studied. The team hopes to finish the project by 2018—300 years after the ship sank.

[1] A **wreck** is a ship that has been destroyed or very badly damaged.

C. Think About It.

1. Do you believe archeologists have really found Blackbeard's ship? How can they know for sure?

2. Why do you think pirates are so popular today?

To learn more about legends of the sea, visit elt.heinle.com/explorer

UNIT 12
Vanished!

Discuss these questions with a partner.

1. Where are the hottest places in the world? The coldest? The highest?
2. Why do you think some people like to visit these extreme places?
3. Would you like to visit any of these places? Why or why not?

▲ Footprints vanish into the sands of Death Valley,
California—one of the hottest places in the world.
Temperatures here have reached 57°C (134°F).

12A On Top of the World

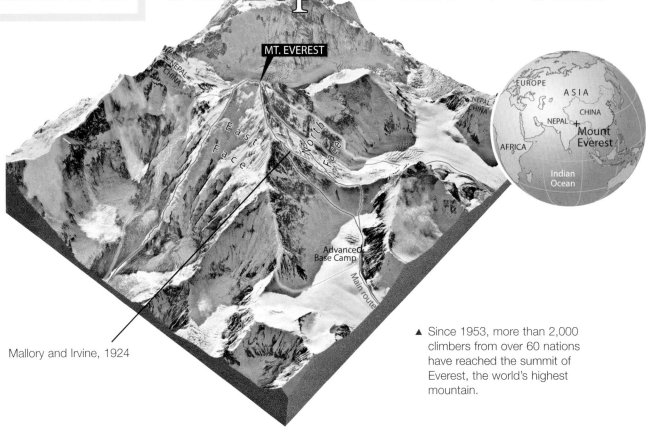

MT. EVEREST

EUROPE ASIA
NEPAL CHINA
CHINA
NEPAL
AFRICA + Mount
Everest
Indian
Ocean

Mallory and Irvine, 1924

▲ Since 1953, more than 2,000 climbers from over 60 nations have reached the summit of Everest, the world's highest mountain.

Before You Read

A. Completion. Complete the information with answers from the box. One answer is extra.

8,850
•
1953
•
oxygen
•
India
•
200
•
Nepal
•
cold
•
4

- *Everest's height:* **1.** _____ meters (29,035 feet); each year, it rises by another **2.** _____ millimeters.

- *First people to reach the summit of Everest:* Tenzing Norgay (a Sherpa from **3.** _____) and Edmund Hillary (from New Zealand), in **4.** _____.

- *Health risks:* Because of the extreme **5.** _____, climbers can get frostbite, especially on their fingers and toes.

- *Equipment:* Most Everest climbers carry **6.** _____ tanks to help them breathe.

- *Number of deaths on Everest:* more than **7.** _____, mostly due to avalanches (large amounts of snow falling down the mountain).

B. Predict. Look at the title and read the first paragraph on the next page. What do you think happened to Mallory and Irvine? Read to check your ideas.

Mystery on Everest

1   Were Edmund Hillary and Tenzing Norgay really the first people to reach the top of Mount Everest? Some believe British climbers George Mallory and Andrew Irvine reached the summit **previously**—
5   in June 1924. Unfortunately, this is hard to **prove** because both men vanished on the mountain.

Recently a team of climbers visited Everest, hoping to solve[1] this mystery. Near Everest's First Step, on the way to the summit, the team found Mallory's
10   oxygen tank—evidence that he and Irvine were near the top. Close by, a member of the team, Conrad Anker, discovered Mallory's body.

▲ Mountain climber Conrad Anker discovered Mallory's body on May 1, 1999.

When the team examined Mallory's body, they found items like a knife and matches, but no photos. Why is this **significant**?
15   Mallory carried a photo of his wife with him. He planned to leave it at the top of Everest, if he reached the summit.

"Because it is there."

—Mallory's response when asked why he wanted to climb Everest

Did Mallory and Irvine **achieve** their goal and reach the top? Probably not, says Anker. Here's why:

Difficult path/Poor equipment: Mallory and Irvine were last
20   seen near Everest's Second Step. This is a 27-meter (90-foot) wall of rock. Climbing this **section** of Everest is extremely difficult, even with modern climbing equipment. Without the right tools, it is **doubtful** Mallory and Irvine were able to **proceed** to the top.

No frostbite: Mallory and Irvine were near the summit late
25   in the day. Climbers who reach the summit at this time need to camp at the top. If you do this, it is common to **suffer** from frostbite. But Mallory's body had no sign of frostbite.

So what happened to Mallory and Irvine? Anker thinks they probably turned back just after the First Step. When Mallory
30   was going down, perhaps he accidentally fell. Irvine's body has never been found. **Whatever** happened, they will always be remembered as early Everest heroes.[2]

▲ Mallory took a camera like this on his climb. It has never been found.

---

[1] If you **solve** a problem, you find an answer to it.
[2] A **hero** is a brave person, someone who does something great.

Reading Comprehension

A. Multiple Choice. Choose the best answer for each question.

Gist **1.** The reading is mainly about two climbers who _____.
   a. solved a mystery about Everest
   b. vanished on Everest
   c. recreated Hillary and Norgay's climb
   d. invented new climbing tools

Detail **2.** Which statement is true?
   a. Mallory and Irvine were last seen near Everest's First Step.
   b. Conrad Anker's team found two bodies on Everest.
   c. Mallory and Irvine were near the top of Everest in the morning.
   d. Anker's team found some of Mallory's things on the mountain.

Reference **3.** In line 16, what does *it* refer to?
   a. the body   c. the summit
   b. the oxygen tank   d. the picture

Vocabulary **4.** If Mallory and Irvine *turned back* (line 29), they _____ the mountain.
   a. stopped and went down   c. tried to walk up
   b. went around   d. stayed in one place on

Inference **5.** Which statement would Conrad Anker probably agree with?
   a. Mallory and Irvine definitely reached the top of Everest.
   b. Mallory and Irvine never got close to the summit.
   c. Mallory and Irvine got close, but didn't reach the top.
   d. Andrew Irvine probably reached the top, but not Mallory.

B. For and Against. Complete the chart with words from the reading. Which side do you agree with?

Did Mallory and Irvine reach the top of Mount Everest?

Reasons for	Reasons against
Conrad Anker's team discovered Mallory's **1.** _____ tank and **2.** _____ near the First Step.	Climbing Everest's Second Step is very **5.** _____, and Mallory and Irvine did not have modern **6.** _____.
The team didn't find a(n) **3.** _____ of Mallory's wife. He planned to **4.** _____ it at the summit.	Mallory's body had no **7.** _____. This is common for people who **8.** _____ near the summit for the night.

134   Unit 12 Vanished!

Vocabulary Practice

A. Completion. Complete the information with the correct form of words from the box. One word is extra.

achieve	doubtful	path	proceed
prove	significant	suffer	

Tenzing Norgay and Edmund Hillary reached the summit of Everest in 1953. But there have been other **1.** _____ "firsts" on Everest since then. Here are two:

- During a climb up Everest in 1975, an avalanche buried Japanese climber Junko Tabei in the snow. It was **2.** _____ that she would survive. Luckily, a group of climbers from Nepal found and saved her. Twelve days later, on May 16, 1975, Tabei **3.** _____ her goal and became the first woman to reach the summit.

- Can a blind[1] person climb Everest? On May 25, 2001, blind American climber Erik Weihenmeyer reached the summit and **4.** _____ it is possible. Three years later, he climbed Everest again with a group of blind teenagers from Tibet. The **5.** _____ to the top of Lhakpa Ri (one of Everest's summits) was difficult. Some teens **6.** _____ from extreme headaches (because of the lack of oxygen). Their amazing journey became a movie called "Blindsight."

[1] A **blind** person cannot see.

▲ In 1999 an avalanche in the Himalayas killed climber Alex Lowe (above, pictured in Antarctica), and badly hurt Conrad Anker— discoverer of Mallory's body.

Did You Know?

Mt. Everest is known in Tibetan as *Chomolungma*. In Nepali, it is called *Sagarmatha*.

B. Words in Context. Complete each sentence with the best answer.

1. If today is Monday, the previous day is/was _____.
a. Tuesday   b. Sunday

2. A newspaper has different sections. This means, it has different _____.
a. colors   b. parts

3. If you proceed in a direction you _____.
a. continue in that direction   b. avoid that direction

4. If you can buy whatever you want, you can buy _____.
a. anything   b. only certain things

Word Link

We can add **–ever** (meaning *any* or *every*) to certain question words (*who, what, where, when*) to form new words. For example, *whenever* means *at any time*.

12B Pioneers[1] of the Sky

▲ In 1997, pilot Linda Finch successfully completed a round-the-world trip, flying in the same kind of plane as Earhart flew in 60 years earlier.

▲ Pilot Amelia Earhart broke many flying records in the 1930s.

Before You Read

A. Discussion. Read the timeline of Earhart's life. How did she become a famous pioneer? What record did she break?

Amelia Earhart (1897–1937)
1918: Sees a small airplane take off in the snow of Toronto, Canada. Decides she wants to fly.
1921: Becomes a pilot at age 24.
May 1932: Breaks a world record: is the first woman to fly a plane alone across the Atlantic Ocean.
May 20, 1937: Wants to be the first woman to fly a plane around the world. Flies with guide Fred Noonan across the U.S.A. from California, south to Brazil, and across Africa, Asia, and Australia.
June 29, 1937: Earhart and Noonan arrive in New Guinea.
July 2, 1937: They take off again, heading for an island in the Pacific Ocean. They are never seen again . . .

[1] A **pioneer** in an activity is one of the first people to do it.

B. Predict. What do you think happened to Earhart and Noonan? Read the passage to check your ideas.

The Missing Pilot

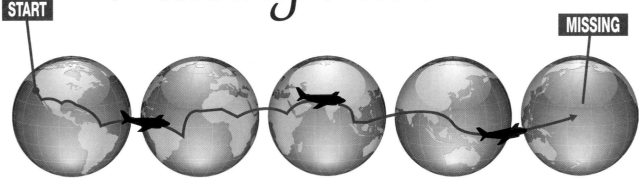

START MISSING

▲ The path of Amelia Earhart's 1937 round-the-world flight

A Dangerous Journey

On July 2, 1937, Amelia Earhart and Fred Noonan left New Guinea for Howland Island in the Pacific. This was the longest and most dangerous part of their trip around the world. Earhart had trouble shortly after takeoff. The weather was stormy, so she had to fly at 3,000 meters (10,000 feet). Going this high, the plane used gas quickly.

After about twenty hours, Earhart and Noonan **approached** Howland Island. The island was only about 105 kilometers (65 miles) away, but the **bright** sun was **shining** in their faces so they couldn't see it. Near Howland, a ship, the *Itasca*, was waiting. Earhart contacted the ship: "Gas is low," she said. The *Itasca* tried to **maintain** contact with her but got no **response**. Finally, the *Itasca* called for help. People searched for Earhart and Noonan for days. Despite the searchers' **efforts**, they found nothing.

Missing!

What happened to Amelia Earhart? No one knows for sure. During the **flight**, she probably **headed** in the wrong direction because the sun was bright and it was hard to see. So she got lost; soon after, her plane ran out of[1] gas, and she died at sea. Another idea is that she survived the plane crash,[2] swam to an uninhabited[3] island, and later died there. Still others think she survived the crash and secretly returned to the U.S. with a new identity.

▲ Not only a pilot, Amelia Earhart was also one of the most stylish women of her time.

Although the first theory seems most likely, none of these ideas has been proven. Today, people are still **investigating** Earhart's and Noonan's **disappearance**. (Noonan's body has also never been found.) Whatever happened, Amelia probably died as she wished. "When I go," she said, "I'd like best to go in my plane."

[1] If you **run out of** something, you have no more of it left.
[2] A **crash** is an accident in which a car, plane, etc. is damaged or destroyed.
[3] If a place is **uninhabited**, it has no people.

Reading Comprehension

A. Multiple Choice. Choose the best answer for each question.

Gist **1.** Another title for this reading could be _____.
  a. Pilot Mystery Is Finally Solved
  b. Amelia Earhart Breaks Another Record
  c. What Happened to Amelia Earhart?
  d. The Last Female Pilot in the U.S.A.

Vocabulary **2.** Why was flying to Howland Island difficult?
  a. Earhart was sick.
  b. Noonan didn't have a map.
  c. Their plane was damaged.
  d. It was very far from New Guinea.

Detail **3.** Shortly after taking off from New Guinea, what happened?
  a. Earhart's plane ran out of gas.
  b. There was a bad storm.
  c. Fred Noonan died.
  d. Earhart's plane crashed.

Inference **4.** In line 27, when Earhart says *"When I go . . . ,"* what does *go* mean?
  a. fly   c. leave
  b. die   d. travel

Inference **5.** Which statement would the writer of the passage agree with?
  a. Amelia's plane probably ran out of gas and she died at sea.
  b. It is possible that Fred Noonan killed Amelia Earhart.
  c. Amelia Earhart probably died on an island in the Pacific.
  d. Fred Noonan might still be alive today.

B. Completion. Complete the sentences in the flow chart, using words from the passage. Then tell a partner what happened to Amelia Earhart.

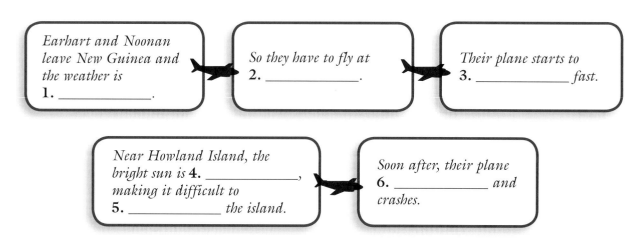

Earhart and Noonan leave New Guinea and the weather is 1. _____.

So they have to fly at 2. _____.

Their plane starts to 3. _____ fast.

Near Howland Island, the bright sun is 4. _____, making it difficult to 5. _____ the island.

Soon after, their plane 6. _____ and crashes.

Vocabulary Practice

A. Completion. Complete the information with words from the box.
One word is extra.

approached	bright	disappearance	efforts	flight
headed	investigate	maintain	response	shine

On September 3, 2007, American adventurer Steve Fossett vanished
in the Nevada desert. Why is Fossett's **1.** _____ so unusual?
Fossett was a skilled pilot, and his **2.** _____ on September 3
wasn't long or difficult. When Fossett didn't return, search planes
3. _____ to the desert to **4.** _____. Despite
their **5.** _____, the missing pilot could not be found.

What happened to Fossett? Maybe the weather caused him to crash.
On September 3, the sun was **6.** _____; it was a beautiful
day. However, Fossett was flying near mountains in the Nevada desert.
Winds here can be dangerous. Maybe it was windy as he
7. _____ the mountains. Perhaps this made it hard to
8. _____ control of his plane and he crashed.

But some things about this story are strange. For example, on September
3, Fossett didn't tell anyone exactly where he was going. Later, people
tried to call his cell phone, but they got no **9.** _____. Fossett
didn't take his phone with him that day. The question is . . . why? As with
Amelia Earhart, we may never know how this story ends.

▲ Hot-Air Pioneer:
In 2002, Steve
Fossett was the
first person to fly
non-stop around
the world in a
balloon by
himself.

B. Definitions. Use the correct form of the words in the box in **A** to complete the definitions.

1. If you _____ someone or something, you try to find out the truth about them.

2. A(n) _____ is a trip you take by plane.

3. A(n) _____ is an answer or reply.

4. If you _____ someone or something, you come closer to it.

5. When the sun or other light _____, it gives out a bright light.

6. If you _____ something, you keep or continue it so it does not change.

7. A(n) _____ is when someone or something vanishes.

8. If you make a(n) _____ to do something, you try very hard to do it.

9. If you _____ to a certain place, you go to that place.

Word Link We can add **dis-** to some words to show an opposite
meaning. For example, if something *disappears*, you
can no longer see it. If you *dislike* someone, you don't like him or her.

EXPLORE *C* **MORE**

Marfa Lights

Marfa, Texas

A. Preview. Read the paragraph below. Can you think of another example of a natural phenomenon?

A *phenomenon* is something that happens or exists. We can see, hear, or feel it. Sometimes, it seems amazing or unusual to us. Some examples of natural phenomena are lighting, rainbows, earthquakes, and fire.

B. Summarize. Watch the video, *Marfa Lights*. Then complete the summary below using the correct form of words from the box. Two words are extra.

achieve	bright	disappear	flight
investigate	maintain	proof	response
section	shine	whatever	

The Chihuahuan desert in West Texas is home to a mysterious phenomenon called the "Marfa Lights." These are
1. _____ lights that appear suddenly in the night sky. Then, just as quickly, they **2.** _____. There are often two or more lights. They appear in the same
3. _____ of the desert—near a town called Marfa. Sometimes they get close to people's houses and
4. _____ through the windows. While training in the desert, pilots have also seen these mysterious lights during their **5.** _____.

What causes the lights? One pilot, Fritz Kahl, has a(n)
6. _____ to this question. He says that the lights are a natural phenomenon. They exist all over the world. But this answer isn't enough for some people. They continue to
7. _____ the lights. They want to know: where exactly do the lights come from? How long have they existed? These people want **8.** _____, not opinions.
9. _____ these lights really are, they are as mysterious today as when they first appeared.

C. Think About It.

1. What do you think causes the Marfa Lights?

2. Are there any famous mysteries from your country?

 To learn more about unexplained mysteries, visit elt.heinle.com/explorer

A. Crossword. Use the definitions below to complete the missing words.

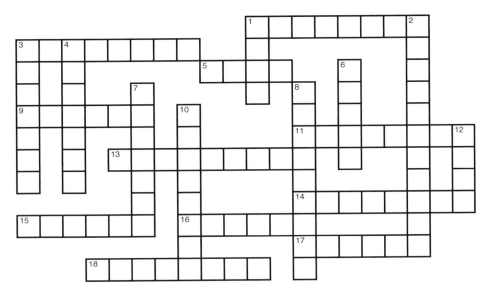

Across
1. not afraid at all
3. to come closer to a person or place
5. to travel somewhere by boat
9. your earnings
11. to move something from one place to another
13. something you build
14. to buy something
15. to rule or control, usually a country
16. something that affects a decision or situation; a reason
17. a specialist in a certain subject
18. forever the same; not of a particular time or date

Down
1. to be unsuccessful at something
2. important
3. to succeed in doing something
4. to go forward
6. to wrongfully take something from another person
7. one part of something
8. to understand or decide the meaning of something
10. unlikely to happen
12. one's job or position

B. Notes Completion. Scan the information on pages 142–143 to complete the notes.

Field Notes

Site: Mausoleum of the First Qin Emperor

Location: Xi'an, _____

Information:
- Army of terracotta warriors discovered in the year _____
- Built over _____ years ago by Chinese _____ Qin Shihuang
- Number of workers who built the structure: _____
- Mausoleum area is about _____ square km
- Became World Heritage Site in _____
- Qin Shihuang also responsible for the first of China's _____
- Tomb still unopened—may have _____ of mercury inside
- 1998: archeologists found 12 statues of _____

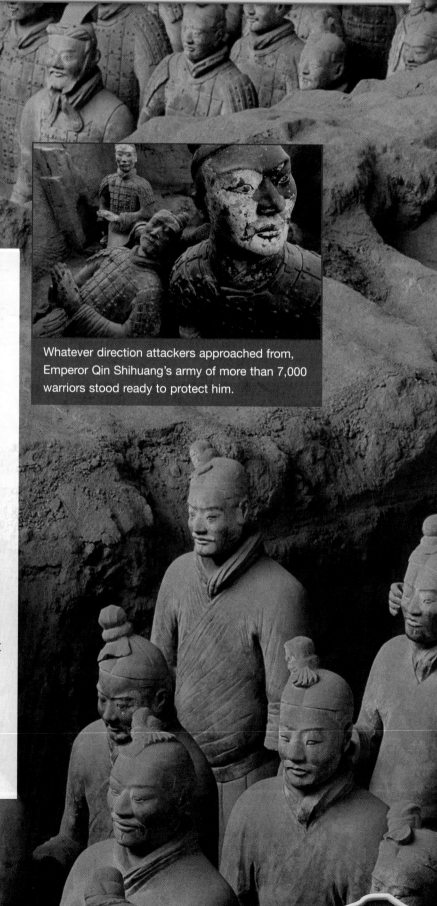

Site: **Mausoleum of the First Qin Emperor**

Location: **Xi'an, China**

Category: **Cultural**

Status: **World Heritage Site since 1987**

Xi'an, China

In 1974, local farmers in the Shaanxi Province of China made an amazing discovery: a huge army of buried warriors. The soldiers, each a life-size statue, had been hidden for more than 2,200 years, silently protecting their leader's tomb.

When uncovered, the statues were standing in the exact position of a real army. Experts have since learned much from them about the fighting strategies of ancient China. Today, this fearless army also stands as a world-famous artistic wonder. Each statue was made by hand and has a unique face. Most likely, their bodies were once entirely painted in bright colors.

The terracotta warriors are part of the giant mausoleum of Emperor Qin Shihuang. The entire structure, 57 square kilometers (22 square miles), is still being unearthed. In addition to his army, experts believe the Emperor had a whole timeless town of people and animals around him in death.

Whatever direction attackers approached from, Emperor Qin Shihuang's army of more than 7,000 warriors stood ready to protect him.

Glossary

mausoleum: a place for a tomb
mercury: a silver metal which, as a liquid, is used in thermometers to measure temperature
terracotta: brown-red clay, used for making objects such as flower pots, roof tiles, and statues

The First Emperor

Emperor Qin Shihuang, a proud leader who ruled from 221 B.C. to 210 B.C., was the first emperor to govern a united China. Over 700,000 people were involved in the construction of his mausoleum. Among his many other achievements, the Emperor was responsible for building the first of China's great walls.

Secrets of the Tomb

Emperor Qin Shihuang's giant tomb has not yet been opened, as archeologists are worried that air and light may damage the objects in the tomb and perhaps the Emperor's body. No one knows exactly what is inside, but ancient texts say that the tomb is designed to look like a city, with rivers of mercury and a sky that shines with treasures. One day, experts hope to investigate the truth of these legends. Until significant advances in technology have been achieved, however, Emperor Qin Shihuang's tomb remains untouched.

The Emperor's Entertainers

In 1998, 12 statues with more playful expressions than the Emperor's soldiers and officials were found at the mausoleum. According to experts, these statues, including this headless acrobat (pictured), were apparently based on real-life entertainers who performed for the Emperor and his family.

A. Word Link. The suffixes **–ful** (meaning "full of") and **–less** (meaning "without") can be added to nouns to form adjectives, e.g. *fearful*, *fearless*. Read the two paragraphs below, and add *–ful* or *–less* to each word to create the correct adjective. Then answer the questions. Use your dictionary to help you.

Archeologists removed the Egyptian king's body from the tomb. Because the body is over 3,000 years old, the team had to be extremely **1.** care_____. How old was the king when he died? Scientists aren't sure. However, they believe he died a quick and **2.** pain_____ death and did not suffer much. Archeologists are **3.** hope_____ that they will learn more after they examine the body.

Most of the journey from Africa to the Caribbean was **4.** peace_____. For weeks, the *Whydah* saw no other ships. But near the islands of the Bahamas, pirates attacked them. Crew members realized it was **5.** sense_____ to fight. The pirates had weapons and were known to be **6.** heart_____ killers. The pirates stole everything, but the crew didn't care. They were **7.** thank_____ to be alive.

1. Which noun in **1–7** can only be used with *–ful*? _____
2. Which two nouns in **1–7** can only be used with *–less*? _____

B. Word Partnership. Read the passage below and underline six **verb + preposition** combinations, e.g., *compete with*, *pretend to*, *suffer from*. Then use the correct form of the combinations to complete the sentences below.

In the seas of southern Japan, underwater archeologists think they may have discovered the ruins of an ancient city. Some experts believe this sunken city is part of Mu—a mythical land that vanished into the sea 2,000 years ago, possibly after a huge earthquake. According to legend, some people escaped from Mu and traveled to other parts of the Pacific.

Scientist Masaaki Kimura has identified different structures from the ancient city, including (in his opinion) a 5,000-year-old pyramid—maybe the oldest in the world. But other scientists disagree with Kimura's findings. They say the underwater structures are natural rock formations, not a part of an ancient sunken city. Kimura responded to this by saying, "The best way to get an . . . answer . . . is to [collect] more evidence."

1. In the legend of Hansel and Gretel, the two children _____ a terrible witch.
2. While some scientists think *Deinocheirus* was a large dinosaur, other scientists _____ them and think it was a small dinosaur with extremely long arms.
3. If you _____ Mexico, you should be sure to visit Teotihuacán.

Target Vocabulary

Target Vocabulary

Target Vocabulary

1 Monkey College

Narrator:

Monkeys are very intelligent animals.
In fact, some smart monkeys even go to college!
The monkeys at the Monkey Training School in Surat Thani, Thailand, are sent there by farmers to learn an important job: how to pick coconuts from very tall trees.

Trainer Somporn Saewkwo says it takes months for the young monkeys to learn the strategy for picking coconuts. For the first month, he just lets the monkey play. He shows him how to spin a coconut in a box. Then he holds the monkey's hand and encourages him to twist the coconut himself. Later, he brings the monkey to a tree and lets him learn how to pick the coconuts that are ready to eat.

Step by step, the monkey goes higher and higher. The trainer uses a rope to control and direct the monkey's work. The monkey goes left, right, up, and down. When Somporn pulls the rope, the monkey goes faster.

Monkeys have been helping Thai farmers to pick coconuts for more than a hundred years. The monkeys climb trees and twist coconuts with their hands until the fruit falls to the ground. Somporn Saewkwo explains the advantages of using monkeys for this job.

Somporn Saewkwo, Monkey Trainer:

"Nowadays, there are about 12,000 monkeys in Surat Thani that are working to pick coconuts, helping humans. If we climb up those trees, we can fall and die."

Narrator:

The coconut is an important fruit for farmers here. Farmers can earn about two dollars for every hundred coconuts that they bring to market. People buy the fruit on Thai beaches, and it's also used in the country's popular coconut curry. A huge number of coconuts—about two million—are produced each month in Thailand. And many farmers say they couldn't pick the fruit without help from their monkeys.

Pak Dee's three-year-old monkey assists with his work. The monkey picks fruit from Pak's own trees. Pak also lends the monkey to other farmers to earn extra money. The animal is so valuable that Pak never leaves it home alone. The monkey could run away or somebody could take it. Pak Dee describes the system he uses:

Pak Dee, Coconut Farmer

"I tie the monkey to a coconut tree near the house. I give him rice to eat, sometimes with curry. The monkey can live to be 13 years old, so he has ten more years that he can work. I don't need any more monkeys than I have now. I just want to carry on with this monkey for his lifetime."

Narrator:

Farmers say that because the monkeys are so important to them, most are well cared for and don't have a hard life. But some people make the animals work too hard and treat them badly.

Somporn Saewkwo:

"In the past, everyone was training monkeys in a different way—and some people were hurting the monkeys."

Narrator:

Trainer Somporn Saewkwo created a different, more gentle method of teaching monkeys, which is now used by others at the monkey training college.

Because a lot of Thailand's forests have disappeared, more and more monkeys now need man's help to be able to live.

Somporn Saewkwo:

"All the monkeys that come to stay with us have a better living than in the jungle. One side does not have an advantage over the other."

Narrator:

As long as Thailand continues to produce coconuts, these farmers will probably continue to use monkeys. You see, the monkey and the coconut will be together always. As long as you have the coconut, you will also have the monkey.

Land Divers

Narrator:

At first, the activity looks familiar, like a traditional form of bungee jumping. But after watching the first diver fall to the earth, it's clear that what's happening here on Pentecost Island is very different.

This is the Naghol, an ancient religious event which means "land diving." The diver's goal is to touch the earth with the top of his head. The people believe this will make sure the earth produces lots of food this year.

The land divers jump from a 21-meter high tower, built in a space in the jungle. From here you can see the Pacific Ocean.

One of the event's organizers, Renee, gives this advice:

Renee, Land Diver:

"Whenever you are on the tower ready to jump, if you have second thoughts, that means you must not jump."

Narrator:

The first diver greets the people. His dive goes well. He hits the ground hard, but he's okay. His friends quickly free him from the vines that are tied to his feet.

The second dive doesn't go as well. The young boys ask about the strength of the vines. But the older divers tell them that they will be strong enough.

But they aren't strong enough.

One of the vines breaks, and the young boy goes face first into the earth. Everyone goes to help him. But the boy doesn't speak; he's hurt.

The last time a land diver was killed here was in 1974. But people get hurt every year—sometimes seriously.

The other boys and men put cold water on the boy's head. Eventually he walks away, assisted by friends and brothers.

One of the older men jumps next. It's an especially good dive—perfect!

People from abroad are not allowed to take part in land diving, as it's only for native divers. But the chief says that a Western cameraman can tie a small camera to a diver's leg. It's the first time this has been done. The people love it. The cameraman thanks the land diver.

Narrator:

The young man who wore the camera on his dive tells about his jumps in the local language, Raga.

Land Diver:

"The first dive was great. The second dive I broke a vine. But as long as I'm not hurt, everything is going well. I'm a lucky man."

Narrator:

The last dive of the afternoon is by one of the best divers on Pentecost Island. He's been diving for many years. He dives from the tower and lands safely. Everyone is very happy.

When it's finished, the children run around the tower. They dream of the day when they'll be old enough to dive, old enough to test their bravery in one of the most unusual events on Earth.

3 | Steel Drums

Narrator:

The islands of the Caribbean region are famous for their relaxing beaches and lively music. But the music of the instrument known as *steelband*, or *pan*, is native to only one island nation: Trinidad and Tobago—home of the steelband.

Steelband music is a popular part of life here. From the small fishing villages to the hilltops, the whole population knows and loves the national instrument.

Tony Poyer, Steelband Expert:

"Pan is most important to Trinidad and Tobago. It's part of our culture. It was invented in Trinidad and Tobago . . . It is the only musical instrument invented in the 20th century."

Narrator:

The special sound brings happiness to children and adults alike, and to musicians from many different places and backgrounds. Through the islands' streets and markets, you can't escape the music.

Where does steelband music come from? Trinidad is an oil-producing nation. During World War II, the island's old oil drums became useful for something else—as musical instruments. The drums produced sounds that have heavily influenced the music of the region, and can now be heard in everything from island calypso to classical music.

In fact, the music goes back several centuries to early Africans who were not allowed to use their own drums.

Tony Poyer:

"They were banned from beating the Congo drums because people thought they were communicating."

Narrator:

At first, people played these African rhythms by hitting old tin cans. Later, people played on the tops of steel drums, and that's how the steelband sound was eventually formed.

Steel drum musicians usually play by ear. Most players don't use music written on paper.

Tony Poyer:

"In fact, in the early days they knew nothing about music. They played by sound, they even tuned the pan by sound—tonk, tonk, tonk—and they listened to the note until they got it right."

Narrator:

The steelband sound starts with the man who tunes the drums—the tuner.

This tuner is known as Honey Boy. He's been tuning pans for many years. It takes a long time to tune the drums. But these instruments are used by some of the region's top performers.

But the steelband is more than just music to Trinidad. It is a part of the local culture, showing the world the creativity of the island's people.

Every night, places called *panyards* fill with musicians who come to learn the instrument. People like Beverly and Dove.

Beverly:

"Well it's the music of my country so . . . I should learn it. I should know a little bit about it."

Dove:

"Pan is to Trinidad part of our main culture. This is ours. We made it, we created it."

Narrator:

Dove says that steelband belongs to the people of Trinidad and Tobago. But it is something which they are happy to share with audiences and musicians around the world.

The Moon

Narrator:

Since ancient times the moon has been a cause of wonder. People once thought it was made of cheese, or was the home of "the man in the moon." Some even thought it could turn people into strange beings called werewolves.

The moon is just one quarter the size of Earth. But for us on Earth the moon looks very big in the night sky. This is because it's only 386,000 kilometers away, a short distance compared with the hugeness of space.

Many scientists believe the moon formed about 4.6 billion years ago.

One idea is that a huge rock, called an *asteroid*, hit Earth so hard that smaller rocks and other material were knocked loose and started to circle the Earth. Eventually, this cloud of rock and material came together to form the moon.

The moon doesn't have much atmosphere to protect it, so it gets hit by a lot of debris from space. Because of this, its entire surface has many thousands of holes, called *craters*.

The scientist Galileo got the first close look at the moon, through his telescope in 1609.

But by the mid-20th century, simply looking at the moon was not enough; we wanted to explore it.

President John F. Kennedy:

"We choose to go to the moon in this decade and do the other things, not because they are easy, but because they are hard."

Narrator:

On July 20, 1969, two American astronauts, Neil Armstrong and Buzz Aldrin, walked for the first time on the moon's surface. The journey was one of the greatest advances in human history.

Neil Armstrong, U.S. Astronaut:

"That's one small step for man, one giant leap for mankind."

Narrator:

Since the moon only has one-sixth the gravity on Earth, the astronauts felt very light on its surface.

The moon circles the Earth in the same way that the Earth goes round the sun.

The moon doesn't shine on its own. Instead, it shines back, or reflects, light from the sun. So on Earth we see more or less of the moon, depending on its position. These views are called "phases."

When the moon is on the far side of the Earth, away from the sun, the moon is full. As the moon circles the Earth, we can only see the sunlight that hits part of it. This creates "crescent moons" or "half moons." When the moon is exactly between the Earth and the sun, light falls on the far side of the moon. Then the moon is dark, or "new."

It takes about 29 days for the moon to complete its cycle. Sometimes, the Earth comes exactly between the sun and a full moon. Sunlight can't reach the moon, creating a total lunar eclipse.

The moon has a powerful influence on our planet. As Earth turns, the moon's gravity pulls our oceans. This creates the movement of the oceans, called tides. The force of the tides has helped shape Earth's coasts and has influenced the rhythms of life.

Our nearest neighbor in space is much more than a beautiful view.

5 Living in Venice

Narrator:
It is early morning in Venice. Before the light of the sun fills the famous Piazza San Marco, the traders of Venice are getting ready for the crowds of tourists. In a few hours, thousands of people will come to this square. But for now, the people of Venice have the city to themselves. Market traders welcome the first visitors.

Market trader (Italian):
"Signori, buon giorno."

Narrator:
Early morning is the best time for shopping in the outdoor markets.

Gino Penzo, Venice Trader:
"We have many, many kinds of fish."

Narrator:
This is the part of Venice that most visitors never see. This is the Venice that some people call home. Resident Fabrizio Copano says that he lives in the most beautiful city in the world. It's a city that's clean and easy to live in, with a high quality of life. But for some people, Venice has disadvantages too.

Gino Penzo:
"My son, he doesn't love, uh, live in Venice. I am very sorry."

Narrator:
The population of Venice is getting increasingly older. Why? Fabrizio says living in Venice is not cheap. Property is particularly expensive, and housing prices have increased a lot in recent years. It's especially difficult for young people looking for their own place to live. Many of them must move away, leaving Venice to the tourists.

It seems like the whole world has come here to the Piazza San Marco. The tourists come to experience a city that feels like it's still in the 15th century. And some local people say that's the problem.

Giovanni dal Missier, Venice Resident:
"Venice did change a lot since I was born."

Narrator:
Giovanni dal Missier is one of the younger people trying to stay in his home town. During the day, the huge crowds of visitors can make just getting home from work very difficult.

Giovanni dal Missier:
"I get bored with the people, with the tourists, because there are too much, too many."

Narrator:
Jobs are another problem. Do you want to be a gondolier or work with tourists? If not, it can be difficult to earn a living here. But some say that the young people leaving Venice will soon find that other cities are not so different.

Gino Penzo:
"Florence is very expensive, Rome is very expensive, London, Paris, Vienna."

Narrator:
It has been said that anyone who comes to Venice will fall in love . . . even if it's only with Venice itself. Giovanni dal Missier knows the feeling. He says that despite all the challenges here, it's hard to think of living anywhere else.

Giovanni dal Missier:
"I know that it's a very special gift that, for me, it's a gift to live in a city such as Venice."

Narrator:
Only a few people get to enjoy living in Venice. These days even fewer people are ready to face the challenges of living here. But for those who stay, it can be a wonderful experience. Every day they can experience the joy of falling in love with Venice all over again.

Silk Weavers of Vietnam

Narrator:

The cocoons of moths have been used to create high quality fabric for over 4,000 years.

A Chinese tradition says that it was discovered by Empress Hsi Ling-Shih. When a cocoon fell into her teacup, the Empress discovered a long thin fiber of silk.

The royal families of China loved silk and thought it was worth more than gold. The secret of its production was kept by China for 2,500 years. It is said that eventually the secret was taken away by a Chinese princess. One day the princess left to get married in India. In her hair she hid some silkworm caterpillars and mulberry seeds for their food.

In the Vietnamese town of Vong Nguyet, silk-making has been an important business for 1,200 years. Many of the village people keep silkworms in their living rooms. Each basket contains hundreds of silkworm caterpillars.

This is the young, or larval, stage of a moth called *Bombyx mori*. Taking care of these caterpillars is hard work. The caterpillars have to eat every two hours during the day and every three hours throughout the night. They eat only mulberry leaves. The caterpillars live only three weeks, and spend all their time eating.

After three weeks, the caterpillars are placed on tree branches. Here, they begin to spin their cocoon. They create this cocoon to protect themselves as they turn into adult moths. First the caterpillar creates a loose pattern of fibers. Eventually, it becomes closed off from the world.

The silk fibers come from a part of the caterpillar's mouth called the salivary glands. The insect spins its head around and an unbroken silk fiber comes out. This fiber ranges from 400 to 600 meters long. To complete the cocoon the caterpillar doesn't stop working for three days.

The silk farmers cannot allow the caterpillar to become an adult moth. If it did, it would eat its way out, and the silk would be broken. The cocoons must be brought to the spinning house before the cycle is complete.

Throughout the village of Vong Nguyet, people turn the cocoons into silk thread. The first step is to heat the cocoons so that the silk becomes loose. The end of each cocoon must be found by hand and spun together. Usually a single thread needs ten or more cocoons.

Vu Thi has been making silk for many years, and is continuing a long tradition.

Vu Thi, Silk Maker:

"Making silk is good work because it is the work of the ancestors. The silk being spun here is done in the old way, as it has been for many years. This machine over here makes it in the new way."

Narrator:

The old spinning machines haven't changed much for over a thousand years. The modern machine next to them has been designed for a finer, higher quality silk thread. It is much faster, but the ends of the silk fibers still have to be found by hand. Once the silk thread is made, it will leave Vong Nguyet and be sent to the weaving town of Van Phuc. Here the silk is made ready for the weaving machines, called looms. Small buildings here have machines from the 1940s.

The process of weaving silk is very slow and the machines must be watched all the time. It takes around two and a half hours to make one meter of silk material. After a lot of work on the part of man and moth, the silk cloth is finally completed. Despite the invention of cheaper materials, natural silk is still loved for its beauty and comfort. This amazing product of man and moth continues to be extremely popular around the world.

7 Dinosaur Discovery

Narrator:

Outside a quiet town in Mexico called Sabinas, there's been an amazing discovery—the remains of a very large dinosaur.

Jose Gonzalez, Ecologist:

"This is a very important thing, the dinosaur is around 50 feet long, 15 feet high; it might weigh between three and four tons."

Narrator:

Jose Gonzalez says that the discovery tells us that the land here, 75 million years ago, was a jungle. Today it is a desert. How did the climate change? Scientists are seeking an answer to this mystery.

In Sabinas, the discovery of the huge dinosaur has created a lot of interest, especially among local children. Some of them were looking for ancient tools used by hunters. Instead, they found dinosaur bones.

Rodrigo Zapata Lozado:

"I was with my dad. He was telling me a dinosaur had been found. We went over there and I found a piece of leg bone."

Daniel Guajardo Ortega:

"When I come out here, I bring the things I need to dig. When I find something that looks like a fossil, I take it to someone so they can tell me if it's a fossil or not."

Narrator:

News of the dinosaur find has spread quickly. Dinosaur bones have now been found at 13 places. And the news has extended to the rest of the world. International paleontologists have come here to examine the giant animal known as *Sabinasaurio*.

Juan Pablo Garcia, a local engineer, first found part of the ancient fossil when he was examining land for construction. He says he was very lucky to find the pieces. He found a circular rock and some other bones, but he didn't know what they were. Garcia had found pieces of the animal's back bone, a leg bone, and other smaller bones. Now, people are searching for the rest . . .

Scientists estimate this could be the most complete dinosaur skeleton ever found in Latin America.

Jose Gonzalez:

"These right here are part of the ribs, these are the vertebrae, OK? We're talking about this is the neck, the cervical vertebrae, right here you have the body of the animal, the back of the animal, we have around 52 to 53 vertebrae total, and right here starts the tail of the animal."

Narrator:

This isn't the first time fossils have been found here. But the appearance of these fossils means that Sabinas has become an important place for dinosaur hunters.

The mayor of Sabinas says that the fossils should be kept in a museum. In his opinion, people from all over Mexico—and abroad—should be able to study the area.

The town's residents feel good that the discovery happened in their town. The group of local people working on the find has grown to more than 60 members.

The mayor says that the discovery has been great for the town.

Local people say the dinosaur discovery has changed their city. They hope that, in the future, more and more dinosaur lovers will visit their region of Mexico.

Sleepy Hollow

Narrator:
In the hills of New York's Hudson River Valley lies Sleepy Hollow—a town known primarily for a very scary legend . . .

The Dutch came to Sleepy Hollow in the 1600s, and started to farm the land. At this old house, you can still see what life was like in the 17th and 18th centuries. You can see farm carts and horses, and learn how to cut wood. Although it's a fun place to visit, the town is most famous today for the story of a tall, thin teacher and a horseman with no head. Storyteller Jonathon Kruk explains the legend:

Jonathon Kruk, Storyteller:
"Now dwelling in these parts, in a tenant house, was a certain schoolmaster by the name of Ichabod Crane."

Narrator:
American author Washington Irving visited this area as a youth. Later he wrote "The Legend of Sleepy Hollow" about the people and places in this town. Bill Lent looks after the Old Dutch Church in Sleepy Hollow. He explains how the story started.

Bill Lent, Sexton Old Dutch Church:
"Grandpas were the entertainment center around the fireplace in the evening."

Narrator:
Bill says the old storytellers created the shocking legend to help keep the kids under control. Bill knows everything about the story, and shows tourists where the famous characters are buried.

Bill Lent:
"And when he was writing the book, he remembered the name on the stone: Katrina Van Tassel—lead female character in 'The Legend of Sleepy Hollow.'"

Narrator:
In the story, the teacher, Ichabod Crane, rode his horse toward this bridge by the Old Dutch Church, racing from the headless horseman.

Jonathon Kruk:
"Ichabod urged his horse, Gunpowder, on, 'come, come,' but the horse needed no further urging as he took off and headed down to get to that churchyard bridge."

Narrator:
At "The Horseman" restaurant, the locals say they love hearing the legend.

Carmen Cruz, Sleepy Hollow Resident:
"So many times I ask myself, is it real or just a legend?"

Narrator:
Every year Sal Tarantino plays the headless horseman in the town's Halloween festival.

Sal Tarantino, Headless Horseman:
"The hardest problem is a real jack-o-lantern. We've tried that several times. A good-sized jack-o-lantern with the right candle in it weighs about 20 pounds. And to hold that out on your arm and try to control the horse at 40 miles per hour in the dark doesn't work too well."

Narrator:
Irving did not actually write the legend here in Sleepy Hollow. But he was deeply affected by the town, and as an adult returned to live here in this large house by the Hudson River. In the house is a complete collection of books written by Irving, including his famous short stories. Today, you can come to visit Irving's house by train. The manager here says that Irving wasn't pleased when the train first arrived, because of the pollution and the noise. When the trains came, things began to change immediately. In 1899 the country's first car factory was built in Sleepy Hollow. The factory recently closed down. But the town is still busy.

Nearly two centuries after Irving wrote "The Legend of Sleepy Hollow," people still find this place magical. And the legend lives on even today. The storyteller says that, if you listen, you may still recognize the sounds of the headless horseman of Sleepy Hollow . . .

9 | Wildfire Photographer

Narrator:

This is where photographer Mark Thiessen likes to spend his vacation . . .

Mark Thiessen,
***National Geographic* Photographer:**

"For me it's an adventure. All of your senses just come alive when you're in the middle of photographing a fire."

Narrator:

Mark says his occupation as a *National Geographic* photographer is not always as exciting as you might think. He spends most of his time taking photos of things like dinosaur bones, or people. He doesn't get to photograph things like dangerous wild animals. But instead of running after wild animals, Mark runs after wildfires.

He tells the story of how he became a photographer as a child.

Mark Thiessen:

"I knew I wanted to be a photographer since I was a little kid."

Narrator:

As a child, Mark would listen to police radio messages at night. When he heard of a fire, he would wake up his mom and they would race to see it.

Mark Thiessen:

"I guess once you get bit by the bug, even at a young age, you just never want to stop."

Narrator:

So every summer, Mark takes his photographic equipment and drives west to photograph wild fires.

This year his first stop is the state of Idaho, where wild fires occur frequently. On this night Mark gets lucky. He rides along through a huge fire that is spreading across the Idaho desert.

Mark Thiessen:

"It's like a tornado going across the front of the truck."

Narrator:

Why is Mark so interested in these fires? He says one of the reasons is that you never know what's going to happen next. That makes it interesting, but also dangerous, sometimes terrifying.

A powerful wind is blowing, and pushes against the truck. To the left, a huge wall of fire is advancing in Mark's direction. It's best to keep moving. The fire can act in strange ways. On his left, Mark can see a "fire whirl." That's when some of the flames start twisting together, creating a fire tornado that can reach a height of ten meters.

Mark is in fact a skilled and capable wildland firefighter himself. His goal is to photograph the men and women who have the tough responsibility of fighting this kind of fire.

Mark Thiessen:

"There's great people to meet who have great stories to tell and great pictures to be taken."

Narrator:

When Mark is with the firefighters, he feels part of a team—a team that's employed to do a very important job. And of course, he is always trying to find the best photographs of the fire.

Although Mark knows that fires have the potential to destroy a lot of land, he is also amazed by their great beauty. He says the sight of trees damaged by fire can be quite beautiful, almost magical.

The opportunity to see and photograph something special brings Mark Thiessen back to the fires every summer. Every time he finishes taking photographs of a fire, he feels tired but also excited. He feels that he's really been alive. And it's clear he plans to continue for many years to come.

Giza Pyramids

Narrator:

Giza. Home of the Pyramids, one of the Seven Wonders of the Ancient World. Tourists from all over the world come to Egypt to visit these amazing structures. But some people are worried.

Zahi Hawass, Archeologist:

"It's like a zoo. I mean the Pyramids, which contain one of the seven wonders of the world— the only one that still exists—to be as though it's like a zoo . . . It's a crime."

Narrator:

A zoo? For archeologist Zahi Hawass, the problem is that around the Pyramids there are camels and horses everywhere. There are also crowds of people competing to sell souvenirs to the tourists. It's difficult, he says, for ordinary visitors to feel how magical and mysterious the Pyramids really are.

Zahi Hawass is leader of the expert archeological team responsible for maintaining the Giza Pyramids. He plans to bring back the ancient wonder of the Pyramids and protect them from the physical damage caused by tourism. He says if this task isn't done now, the Pyramids could disappear in a hundred years.

Giza is home to the most famous ancient monuments in the world— the Great Pyramid of Khufu, his son Khafre, and grandson Menkaure. And watching over all three—the Great Sphinx.

Egyptians are proud of these timeless monuments. But moving closer to the Pyramids are the houses of Cairo residents, approaching from all directions. According to Hawass, the houses seem to be "attacking," almost killing, the Pyramids.

Zahi Hawass:

"I always say the Pyramids can never be killed. Now it can be killed."

Narrator:

Giza is home not only to the Pyramids, but more than four million people. It's a large, crowded suburb, an area just outside Cairo, with lots of noise and traffic. Even though officials can't just bring the buildings down, they can stop the city getting closer by building this . . . a wall.

Hawass says the wall is designed primarily to control the number of people entering the Pyramids site. It's a wise development, he says. The role of the wall is to protect tourists from all the camels and horses, and to keep the area of the Pyramids more peaceful. Visitors, as Hawass says, will now be able to feel the magic of the Pyramids in their heart.

The Giza Project is also finding and protecting a number of ancient objects. Although not as famous as the giant Pyramids, these smaller tombs are also being carefully protected.

Laborers here are finding and working with the artifacts. One day, sites like this one will be open to tourists. This will take away traffic and stress from the three big Pyramids and the Sphinx.

Even after centuries of digging and discovering amazing monuments in Giza, the team are still making new discoveries.

You never know, says Hawass, what secrets are here. He believes that, across the centuries, the kings of Egypt are saying thank you to today's Pyramid protectors.

11 | Blackbeard's Cannons

Narrator:

At sunrise, off the Carolina coast . . . the waters are blood red . . . like pirate's blood.

In 1717, Blackbeard the pirate captured a French slave ship. He renamed it the *Queen Anne's Revenge*. For a year, Blackbeard's terrifying group of pirates sailed in this ship. But in 1718, the ship disappeared. What happened? Did the terrible and fearless Blackbeard sink it himself? Nobody is sure, but archeologists are finding clues to the mystery.

Archeologist Kim Eslinger looks at a map where they think the ship is. For five years, archeologists have been studying the remains of a shipwreck found about a kilometer from the coast. They know that most of the ship's wooden body is gone. But its large guns—its cannons—are still there.

It's difficult for the archeologists to see far in the dark water. They put ropes around one of the cannons, so they can pull it up to the surface. Their hope is that on the cannon they will find a name— *Concorde*—the original name of the French ship that Blackbeard stole.

Mike Daniel is the maritime historian who discovered the remains. He's sure they have identified Blackbeard's ship.

Mike Daniel, Naval Historian:

"Most of the evidence on the site points to the fact that it is the *Queen Anne's Revenge*. I'm a hundred percent sure, due to the fact that it is where it was supposed to be."

Narrator:

Everything that archeologists have found is dated before 1718—the year that Blackbeard's ship disappeared.

When the cannon is eventually pulled out of the water, it doesn't look much like a cannon at all. It looks dirty and strange after almost 300 years under water. To project boss Mike Ramsing, the cannon is ugly, but also beautiful.

Mike Ramsing, Project Director:

"Well it doesn't look like much but I'm pretty certain it's at least one cannon . . ."

Narrator:

For him, it's the most important find in years.

Mike Ramsing:

"This is the highlight of my career here."

Narrator:

When the archeologists eventually clean it up, they'll be able to get a closer look at the find. Until then, they use special X-ray technology originally developed for the army to look at the cannon inside. Archeologist Kim Eslinger explains why it's important to X-ray first:

Kim Eslinger, Archeologist:

"It helps us with our research, helps us as we start to break into things, you never just want to sort of break into it and not know what you're going to expect."

Narrator:

Another project archeologist, Wayne Lusardi, says that it may take two months to get all the rocks off of the cannon and to carefully study and record each layer of information. Lusardi says that the cannon will be transferred to a special bath. This will take off the salt and make sure that the metal will survive in the air. That may take two or three years. It's a long wait to see if the cannon has the name that the team has been searching for.

The team would like to finish the project by the year 2018, 300 years after the *Queen Anne's Revenge* disappeared.

Kim Eslinger:

"To open one of these up and find the definitive proof that it is definitely Blackbeard's ship would be probably pretty overwhelming,"

Narrator:

The archeologists hope that one day they will confirm this really is the *Queen Anne's Revenge*—the ship that was sailed 300 years ago by the terrifying pirate known as Blackbeard . . .

Marfa Lights

Narrator:
In the desert of West Texas, there's not a lot of activity. It's hot and dry, and not many people live here.

But on this ancient land there is a mystery. And the best place to see this mystery is at the viewing site, just east of Marfa on the highway called U.S. 90. From here, on almost any night, you can watch the mysterious Marfa Lights.

What do the lights look like? Well, it depends on who you talk to.

One Marfa resident talks about the first time she saw them:

Sherri Eppenauer, Marfa Resident:
"I remember the night well that I saw the Marfa Lights for the first time."

Narrator:
They appeared suddenly, she says, and were very fast. They divided into two bright lights, then into four.

Sherri Eppenauer:
"I've seen them several times, but they never appear the same way. Each time they're a little different when I see them."

Narrator:
Another local resident tells her story:

Felicia Wood, Marfa Resident:
"Well, it was about six years ago, and the strangest thing happened to me. I was living out in the Chenocktee Mountains on a ranch out in West Texas, and getting ready to go to bed that evening, got in bed, turned out the lights, and a bright light just showed up . . ."

Narrator:
According to Wood, the light shone through her window, changed colors, and stayed there for a few minutes. Then it headed off into the distance.

The appearance and disappearance of the lights was seen by pilots flying here many years ago too. Here you can find an old World War II training site. In the mid-1940s, many of the pilots saw the mysterious lights during their flights. Fritz Kahl was one of them.

Fritz Kahl, Marfa Resident:
"We discovered these by chance off in the distance, close to the ground, very small, very soft, and it's a phenomena that they tell me exists over other parts of the world. This happens to be our local chapter of that book, that phenomenon in the mystery world."

Narrator:
But who can explain where the lights come from? Where are they actually located? How long have they existed?

Despite efforts to explain the phenomenon, some are doubtful that these questions will ever be answered.

Another local resident says that the mystery is not a bad thing. If the mystery is unanswered, he says, people will keep investigating, keep looking for the answer.

Whatever these lights really are, their mystery and magic goes on.

Photo Credits

3 Brian J. Skerry/National Geographic Image Collection, 4 (t) Shutterstock, (c) Ralph Lee Hopkins/National Geographic Image Collection, (b) David Alan Harvey/National Geographic Image Collection, 5 (t) O. Louis Mazzatenta/National Geographic Image Collection, (b-l) Mitchell Feinberg/National Geographic Image Collection, (b-r) NASA, 6–7 (b), Sarah Leen/National Geographic Image Collection, 6 (l) istockphoto.com, (t) Tim Laman/National Geographic Image Collection, (b) Shutterstock, (r) Gordon Wiltsie/National Geographic Image Collection, 7 (t) Shutterstock, (t–r) David McLain/National Geographic Image Collection, (r) Ira Block/National Geographic Image Collection, (b–r) Fritz Hoffman/National Geographic Image Collection, (b–c) Cary Wolinsky/National Geographic Image Collection, (b–l) Bill Curtsinger/National Geographic Image Collection, 8 (t) Kenneth Garrett/National Geographic Image Collection, 9 Tim Laman/National Geographic Image Collection, 10 (t, c, b) Shutterstock, 11 (t) Shutterstock, (b) Else Bostelmann/National Geographic Image Collection, 13 (t) Tim Laman/National Geographic Image Collection, (b) Vincent J. Musi/National Geographic Image Collection, 14 Paula Bronstein/Getty Images, 15, 16 William Albert Allard/National Geographic Image Collection, 17 NOVICA.com, 18, 148 Cyril Ruoso/Minden Pictures/National Geographic Image Collection, 19 Stephen Alvarez/National Geographic Image Collection, 20 (t) Stephen Ferry/National Geographic Image Collection, (t–c) Dean Conger/National Geographic Image Collection, (b–c) Frans Lanting/National Geographic Image Collection, (b) Shutterstock, 21 courtesy of RibbonOfRoad.com, 23 (t) Kenneth Garrett/National Geographic Image Collection, (b) Peter Essick/National Geographic Image Collection, 24 (t) Phil Schermeister/National Geographic Image Collection, (c x2) David McLain/National Geographic Image Collection, (b) Brian J. Skerry/National Geographic Image Collection, 25 (t) Gordon Gahan/National Geographic Image Collection, 25 (b), 28, 149 Kal Muller/National Geographic Image Collection, 26 Carsten Peter/National Geographic Image Collection, 27 Joanna B. Pinneo/National Geographic Image Collection, 29 David Alan Harvey/National Geographic Image Collection, 30–31 (t) David Alan Harvey/National Geographic Image Collection, 30 William Albert Allard/National Geographic Image Collection, 31 (b) Shutterstock, 33 David Alan Harvey/National Geographic Image Collection, 34 (l) Stephanie Maze/National Geographic Image Collection, (r) Brooks Walker/National Geographic Image Collection, 35 David Alan Harvey/National Geographic Image Collection, 37 (t) Shutterstock, 38 (l) Shutterstock, 38 (r), 150 Todd Gipstein/National Geographic Image Collection, 39 Shutterstock, 41 (l) Ralph Lee Hopkins/National Geographic Image Collection, (r) Hiram Bingham Jr./National Geographic Images, 42 Abraham Nowitz/National Geographic Image Collection, 43, 44 (t, b), 45 (b) ESA and NASA, 44 (c) photos.com, 45, 47, 48 (t, b), 49 (t), 52, 151 NASA, 49 Jeanne Modderman and Rebecca Hale/National Geographic Image Collection, 51 NASA/JPL-Caltech/University of Arizona, 53 Fritz Hoffman/National Geographic Image Collection, 55 (t, b) Stuart Franklin/National Geographic Image Collection, 57 Shutterstock, 58, 59, 61 Maggie Steber/National Geographic Image Collection, 62, 152 Shutterstock, 63 Bill Hatcher/National Geographic Image Collection, 64 Joel Sartore/National Geographic Image Collection, 65 (t, b) Mitchell Feinberg/National Geographic Image Collection, 66 NASA, 67 (t) O. Louis Mazzatenta/National Geographic Image Collection, (b) Shutterstock, 68 Cary Wolinsky/National Geographic Image Collection, 69 (t, b) Richard Nowitz/National Geographic Image Collection, 71 Michael Yamashita/National Geographic Image Collection, 72, 153 W. Robert Moore/National Geographic Image Collection, 73 (t) H. Edward Kim/National Geographic Image Collection, (b) Justin Guariglia/National Geographic Image Collection, 74 H. Edward Kim/National Geographic Image Collection, 75 (l, r) Justin Guariglia/National Geographic Image Collection, 76 NASA, 77 Robert Clark/National Geographic Image Collection, 78, 82 Pixeldust Studios/National Geographic Image Collection, 79 (t) Robert Clark/National Geographic Image Collection, (c) Doug Henderson/National Geographic Image Collection, (b) Randy Olson/National Geographic Image Collection, 81 O. Louis Mazzatenta/National Geographic Image Collection, 83 (t) Ira Block/National Geographic Image Collection, 85 Jonathan Blair/National Geographic Image Collection, 86, 154 Shutterstock, 87, 88, 92 (t) Gerd Ludwig/National Geographic Image Collection, 89 (t) Landov, 92 (b) Shutterstock, 93 Marc Moritsch/National Geographic Image Collection, 95 Photograph by Farah Nosh, 96, 155 Shutterstock, 97, 99 Carsten Peter/National Geographic Image Collection, 102, 103, 104, 106, 156 Mark Thiessen/National Geographic Image Collection, 105 courtesy of A. J. Coston, 107 Mark Cosslett/National Geographic Image Collection, 108–9 Brian J. Skerry/National Geographic Image Collection, 109 (t, b) Frans Lanting/National Geographic Image Collection, 109 (kiwi) Shutterstock, 110 © 2008 National Geographic, 111 Simon Norfolk/National Geographic Image Collection, 112, 113 Jesus Lopez/National Geographic Image Collection, 114, 116, 117 (t), 118 Kenneth Garrett/National Geographic ImageCollection, 115 Vania Zouravliov/National Geographic Image Collection, 117 (b) Christopher A. Klein/National Geographic Image Collection, 119 Maria Stenzel/National Geographic Image Collection, 120 (l), 157 Martin Gray/National Geographic Image Collection, (r) Richard Nowitz/National Geographic Image Collection, 121 Wes C. Skiles/National Geographic Image Collection, 122 (t) Don Maitz/National Geographic Image Collection, 123 (t) Bill Curtsinger/National Geographic Image Collection, (b) Stephen St. John/National Geographic Image Collection, 125 Brian J. Skerry/National Geographic Image Collection, 126 Stephen St. John/National Geographic Image Collection, 127 Michael Yamashita/National Geographic Image Collection, 130, 158 Robert Clark/National Geographic Image Collection, 131 Dawn Kish/National Geographic Image Collection, 133 (t) Gordon Wiltsie/National Geographic Image Collection, (b) Mark Thiessen/National Geographic Image Collection, 134 Shutterstock, 135 Gordon Wiltsie/National Geographic Image Collection, 136 (t, b), 137 Sarah Leen/National Geographic Image Collection, 139 Joel Sartore/National Geographic Image Collection, 140, 159 Michael Nichols/National Geographic Image Collection, 141, 142–3 O. Louis Mazzatenta/National Geographic Image Collection

Illustration Credits

4–5, 15, 18, 21, 23, 24, 27, 28, 31, 34, 35, 38, 40–41, 54, 55, 58, 62, 72, 86, 89, 91, 96, 106, 113, 116, 120, 122, 129, 130, 132, 140: National Geographic Maps, 137: istockphoto.com

Text Credits

11 Adapted from "Ten Cool Things About Dolphins," by George David Gordon: National Geographic Kids, Jun/Jul 2005, and "The Secret Language of Dolphins," by Crispin Boyer: National Geographic Kids, Jun/Jul 2007, 15 Adapted from "Thailand's Urban Giants," by Douglas H. Chadwick: National Geographic Magazine, Oct 2005, 21 Adapted from "Your Story: Living the Dream," by Gregg Bleakney: National Geographic Adventure, Dec 2006/Jan 2007, 25 Adapted from "Extreme Destination: Yasur Volcano, Vanuatu," by Ted Allen: National Geographic Adventure, Winter 1999, 31 Adapted from "Hip-Hop Planet," by James McBride: National Geographic Magazine, Apr 2007, 35 Adapted from "Where Brazil Was Born: Bahia," by Charles E. Cobb, Jr.: National Geographic Magazine, Aug 2002, 45 Adapted from "Alien Life: Astronomers Predict Contact by 2025," by Hillary Mayell: National Geographic News (http://news.nationalgeographic.com/news), Nov 14, 2003, and "Aliens 'Absolutely' Exist, SETI Astronomer Believes," by Tom Foreman: National Geographic News (http://news.nationalgeographic.com/news), Apr 1, 2003, 49 Adapted from "Space: The Next Generation," by Guy Gugliotta: National Geographic Magazine, Oct 2007, and "Q & A with Robert Zubrin," by Ted Chamberlain: National Geographic Adventure, Sep/Oct 2000, 55 Adapted from "Challenges for Humanity: Cities," by Erla Zwingle: National Geographic Magazine, Nov 2002, and "Urban Downtime," by Jennifer Ackerman: National Geographic Magazine, Oct 2006, 59 Adapted from "Sudden City," by Afshin Molavi: National Geographic Magazine, Jan 2007, 65 Adapted from "Every Shoe Tells a Story," by Cathy Newman: National Geographic Magazine, Sep 2006, 69 Adapted from "The Queen of Textiles," by Nina Hyde: National Geographic Magazine, Jan 1984, 79 Adapted from "New Picture of Dinosaurs Is Emerging," by Hillary Mayell: National Geographic News (http://news.nationalgeographic.com/news), Dec 17, 2002, and "Flesh and Bone," by Joel Achenbach: National Geographic Magazine, Mar 2003, 83 Adapted from "Extreme Dinosaurs," by John Updike: National Geographic Magazine, Dec 2007, 89 Adapted from "Guardians of the Fairy Tale," by Thomas O'Neill: National Geographic Magazine, Dec 1999, 93 Adapted from "The Seven Ravens,": http://www.nationalgeographic.com/grimm/index2.html, 99 Adapted from "The Hard Science, Dumb Luck, and Cowboy Nerve of Chasing Tornadoes," by Priit J. Vesilind: National Geographic Magazine, Apr 2004, 103 Adapted from "Russian Smokejumpers," by Glenn Hodges: National Geographic Magazine, Aug 2002, 113 Adapted from "Pyramid of Death," by A. R. Williams: National Geographic Magazine, Oct 2006, and "New Digs Decoding Mexico's 'Pyramids of Fire,'" by John Roach: National Geographic News (http://news.nationalgeographic.com/news), Oct 21, 2005, 117 Adapted from "The Pyramid Builders," by Virginia Morell: National Geographic Magazine, Nov 2001, 123 Adapted from "Grim Life Cursed Real Pirates of Caribbean," by Stefan Lovgren: National Geographic News (http://news.nationalgeographic.com/news), Jul 11, 2003, and "Pirates of the Whydah," by Donovan Webster: National Geographic Magazine, May 1999, 127 Adapted from "Pirates!": http://www.nationalgeographic.com/pirates/adventure.html, 133 Adapted from "Mystery on Everest," by Conrad Anker: National Geographic Magazine, Oct 1999, and "Out of Thin Air," by David Roberts: National Geographic Adventure, Fall 1999, 137 Adapted from "Amelia Earhart," by Virginia Morell: National Geographic Magazine, Jan 1998, and "Expedition Scours Pacific for Amelia Earhart Wreck," by Jennifer Hile: National Geographic News (http://news.nationalgeographic.com/news), Dec 15, 2003